Psychodietetics

FOOD AS THE KEY
TO EMOTIONAL HEALTH

Psychodietetics

FOOD AS THE KEY
TO EMOTIONAL HEALTH

by E. Cheraskin, M.D., D.M.D.
and W. M. Ringsdorf, Jr., D.M.D., M.S.
with Arline Brecher

STEIN AND DAY/*Publishers*/New York

First published in 1974
Copyright © 1974 by E. Cheraskin, W.M. Ringsdorf, Jr., and Arline Brecher
Library of Congress Catalog Card No. 74-78529
All rights reserved
Designed by David Miller
Printed in the United States of America
Stein and Day/*Publishers*/Scarborough House
Briarcliff Manor, N.Y. 10510
ISBN 0-8128-1725-7

FOURTH PRINTING, 1975

Contents

Acknowledgments

The Optimal Diet and this book have much in common; major foodstuffs are essential, but equally vital are many contributing factors.

The authors are like the most-publicized vitamins, C, E, and A—ineffective without the support of dozens of less recognized nutrients. Vitamin B_3 (niacin), for instance, is one of the important supplements. In the making of this book Carol Cheraskin played the part of B_3, steadying the authors' nerves; Doris Ringsdorf was the sunshine vitamin D; Harold Brecher offered the leveling influence of zinc, sparking creative impulses and subduing erratic ones.

Alda McDowell and Andrea Barclay, our secretaries, acted like calcium and phosphorous, providing the muscle and bone of the manuscript. The trace minerals behind them were Frances Medford and Bradley Hicks, supplying background material.

Like the eight essential amino acids, Dr. Alfred Churchill, Dr. Alan Cott, Dr. David Hawkins, Dr. Abram Hoffer, Dr. Marshall Mandell, Dr. Humphry Osmond, Dr. Linus Pauling, and Dr. Carl Pfeiffer proved indispensable, as were their nutritional research findings.

The essential fatty acids must also be mentioned: Dr. Joseph F. Volker and Dr. Charles A. McCallum are among those at the University of Alabama in Birmingham who have created an atmosphere conducive to our undertaking this and other projects.

Without vitamin B_{12}, people and projects get sluggish. Senior Editor Renni Browne, with the help of her co-enzyme Liz Kelly, kept us to our deadline; like B_{12}, Renni not only "upped" our productivity, but also interacted so well with all the other ingredients that it was she who made the final product digestible.

E. Cheraskin, M.D., D.M.D.
W. M. Ringsdorf, Jr., D.M.D., M.S.
Arline Brecher

Preface

"The beginning of wisdom," says an ancient Chinese proverb, "is to call things by their right name."

No "right name" existed for the new wisdom that is developing as scientists demystify the biochemical pathways which determine psychological functioning. Our first task, then, was to create one.

Psychodietetics is that name. Its roots, *psyche* and *diet*, are familiar. Their union into a noun underscores the close relationship between diet and mental health. It is hoped that once this relationship is made clear, proper diet will become an important tool in the prevention and treatment of mental illness. Such an event presupposes wide recognition of the concept that nutrition has an intimate and intricate influence on personality, mood, and emotions.

Now that there is a name, filling a scientific and linguistic void, we can proceed to wisdom by detailing all the known and suspected ways in which dietary intake is related to emotional health and disease.

The playwright John Patrick once wrote, "Pain makes man think. Thought makes man wise. Wisdom makes life endurable."

Man has suffered pain for too long from emotional problems which have defied treatment. Thoughtful men are providing new antidotes for such pain.

Psychodietetic wisdom promises to make life much more than just "endurable" for all those who are willing to apply to their own lives the nutritional therapy it defines.

9

1

From Food to Mood: What Psychodietetics Is All About

Any important "new idea" has to go through three stages: first ridicule, then discussion, and finally, general acceptance.

Psychodietetics introduces the revolutionary idea that a host of emotional problems, presently mislabeled "mental," are actually rooted in improper diet and nutrition. The concept that emotional complaints can be prevented, treated, and cured by improved nutrition now hovers somewhere between the stages of ridicule and discussion. This book is primarily an effort to accelerate into general acceptance the principle that food nutrients are *the* key to emotional health, so that millions of Americans, beset by a host of misdiagnosed, nutritionally caused emotional ailments, can benefit.

Medical investigators have known for many years that severe nutritional deficiencies cause severe mental illness. In recent years, a number of innovative researchers examining less serious mental conditions have found evidence supporting their suspicion that the twilight zones of emotional distress also are caused or worsened by malfunctions of the body's nutritional machinery. Most recently, a few researchers have discovered that *certain people are genetically predisposed to extra special nutrient needs.*

Based on the mounting evidence that sound biochemical principles underly the food-to-mood phenomenon, and that dietary nutrients have a profound influence on the way we feel, think,

11

respond to, and perceive the world around us, the authors conclude that nutritional therapy should be used as an adjunct to all other forms of mental therapy. In many of the cases we've treated, diet alone "did the trick." In others, various forms of therapy were combined with dietary adjustments to bring long-term patients to full recovery.

The great danger facing the ideas put forth in *Psychodietetics* is not that they will be ridiculed, but that they will be so heartily accepted by a public overanxious for relief from its problems that many will leap to the false conclusion that diet alone can cure all ills.

It cannot.

While the evidence is compelling that innumerable conditions normally termed "psychiatric" are actually cases of metabolic distortion, the ultimate result of poor diet, psychoanalytically oriented therapists need not fear that we propose to replace the psychiatrist's couch with vitamins.

Nutritional therapy does not provide the insight and emotional understanding many people still need once their metabolic imbalances are corrected. Psychological counseling is often necessary to overcome bizarre "learned behaviors" which, after years of nutrient impoverishment, have become inflexible responses to stress. Standard psychological therapy is most valuable when the patient is no longer the victim of distorted metabolic perception—when he is free to accept and act upon the wisdom being offered.

Psychodietetics does show, however, many cases in which a change in diet brought about remarkable recovery on the part of patients suffering from schizophrenia, alcoholism, drug dependency, psychoses, depression, and other serious problems. The fact of these recoveries is certain to bring new hope to other mentally burdened people.

The reports of less seriously troubled people, who are nervous, tense, jittery, overanxious, overweight, underweight, or overtired—*and have been dramatically helped by modifications in diet*—will inspire many to make similar adjustments in the way they eat.

The reader cannot help but gain if he applies the sound nutritional advice found in this book. A person's internal climate is largely responsible for the way the external environment affects his physical and emotional health. For example, only a small percentage of any large group of people breathing the same germ-laden air will catch a cold. In the same way, only a certain proportion of the population at large will suffer emotional collapse because of exposure to "psychic germs," despite the fact that similar stresses and tensions abound in their lives.

What makes the difference between those who are and those who are not felled by the exposure? In *Nutrition Against Disease*, the noted biochemist Roger J. Williams explains that brain cells, like all living cells, are commonly undernourished. "To give them fuller and better balanced nutrition," Dr. Williams points out, "seems like an exceedingly promising way both to prevent and treat mental disease."

In addition to setting forth the great variety of conditions that respond well to nutritional therapy, plus the scientific evidence that explains why this approach will work, *Psychodietetics* offers step-by-step programs for the reader to follow. Some of the questionnaires found in each chapter will help you determine how susceptible you are to emotional collapse. Others will show how your diet can be contributing to such vulnerability.

The reader who, like Thoreau's "mass of men," is living a life of "quiet desperation"—who has found the spark gone out of a marriage, who is often "too tired" to take an interest in sex, sports, or work, who is in constant turmoil because someone he loves is displaying neurotic behavior—is urged to take heart and read on. *Psychodietetics* provides new answers for old problems.

For two and a half decades, the authors have lectured to the health profession, expressing in the proper professional forums many of the same scientifically sound ideas that are expressed in this book. We have been greeted mostly by the polite and courteous nonresponse that health professionals generally reserve for their less orthodox colleagues. This is to be expected: doctors are a product of what they were taught in school. As Dr. Jean Mayer of Harvard University has explained, nutrition is a nonsubject in most medical curricula.

"We have just completed a study to find out what the average doctor at Harvard knows about nutrition," Dr. Mayer said recently. "What we found is this—the average doctor at Harvard knows a wee bit more about nutrition than his secretary, unless his secretary has a weight problem, in which case the average secretary knows a wee bit more about nutrition than the average doctor."

And so we take our case to the public, where it is bound to meet with a more enthusiastic response. If we can influence large numbers of people to provide their brain cells with enough nutrients (minerals, vitamins, essential fatty acids, amino acids, and others) to keep them in reasonably good working order, we have done more to combat *all* known ailments than we could by discovering one more miracle drug.

The forecast by medical prognosticators that some twenty million Americans are headed for a nervous breakdown and untold millions more are doomed to live a shadowy existence interrupted by periodic neurotic or psychotic episodes is a gloomy one indeed. Yet that forecast need not come true. The nation can enjoy a healthier future if we can improve our eating habits.

In his series on *Diet and War*, J. I. Rodale correlated a country's tendency toward either a warlike or a peaceful disposition to its dietary habits. He pointed out that excess consumption of three foods, artificial sugar, wheat and rye products, and meat, seemed always to be accompanied by an aggressive and disputatious national policy.

What, then, of America? According to figures supplied by the Economics Research Service of the Department of Agriculture, the per capita consumption of meat has climbed from 145 pounds per person in 1950 to 161 pounds in 1960 and on to an all-time high of 192 pounds in 1971. At the same time, the per capita consumption of refined sugar has also risen, from 85 pounds in 1920 to the current level of 103 pounds.

Paralleling these documented changes in diet, there has been a devastating escalation in the number of violent crimes reported in the country. In 1940 there were a total of 151,920 incidents of violence on record. The figure almost doubled by 1950, and the most recent data show 828,151 violent crimes on the books for the year 1972.

Without denying the many social and moral changes that have contributed to the rise in violence, we maintain that the nation's deteriorating eating habits share major responsibility.

It is interesting to note that biographers of Adolph Hitler have characterized him as gluttonous in his consumption of sweets, desserts, and heavy meats. Hitler has been described by at least one historian as a "sugar drunkard."

Yet the case for a relationship between diet and behavior does not rest on such extreme examples. There is research supporting a link between nutritional mistakes and almost every imaginable kind of emotional trauma, including depression-induced suicides, automobile accidents, pilot's error, juvenile delinquency, sexual maladjustments, learning difficulties and behavior problems in children, mental retardation, senility, and a long list of more ordinary complaints.

In an article on marriage failures published in a medical magazine, Dr. Cecilia Rosenfeld makes a strong case for nutritional guidance as a major source of help:

One of the prime causes of marital discord—nutritional deficiency—is too often overlooked. In my own practice I have found that in a surprising number of broken marriages, spouses suffered from a blood-sugar imbalance. Many of these husbands and wives showed symptoms of irritability, violent temper, abnormal sensitivity, and extreme fatigue. In most cases, there was no evidence of organic disease. Corrective nutritional guidance dispelled these unpleasant symptoms for many spouses—and, in the process, often bolstered their crumbling marriages.

Dr. Rosenfeld's views are shared by Dr. Joseph Nichols, president of Natural Food Associates and author of the book *Please,*

Doctor, Do Something. "The unhappily married," he believes, "are more often suffering from dietary deficiencies than from the kind of social incompatabilities traditional therapists seek to explore."

Such professional opinions are valuable, without question. Yet evidence from research scientists investigating the cellular and biochemical nature of man's behavior patterns is even more heartening. One such report cropped up recently from Dr. Donald Eccleston, assistant director of the MRC Brain Metabolism Unit of the University of Edinburgh. "The notion that moods can be determined by biochemical defects in the brain may be difficult to accept," Dr. Eccleston has written. "Now, twenty years after the first indications, evidence is accumulating in support of primary biochemical lesions as a cause of a number of psychiatric disorders."

Doctor Eccleston's highly sophisticated discussion of this subject is profoundly important since it verifies the relationship between food and mood *as a metabolic process.*

At this point, ask yourself what problems threaten your serenity or that of your family. A marriage foundering? Alcoholism or drug dependency? A highly rebellious teenager? A neurotic or psychotic relative? Insomnia? Tension? The fear that you may be one of the more than twenty million people in the United States predicted to be heading for a mental breakdown?

Even a partial listing of correlations which have been observed in many patients between diet and psychologic disorders is worth calling to the attention of anyone you care about who has similar complaints:

Nutrient Variable	Behavioral Disorder
subnutrition	depressive psychosis
increased nicotinamide oxidation	schizophrenia
low absorption of vitamin B_{12}	confusion, paranoia, personality disorders
abnormal sodium and potassium metabolism	affective illnesses
sodium retention	psychotic depression
abnormal sodium distribution	melancholia
abnormal sugar metabolism	schizophrenia, depressive psychosis, nonspecific depression, alcoholism, manic psychosis, anxiety, irritability, fatigue, mental confusion, uncontrolled emotional outbursts
abnormal ascorbic acid metabolism	schizophrenia
abnormal vitamin B_6 metabolism	depression

The encouraging news is this: you need not wait until you suffer such obvious emotional distress before benefiting from the psychodietetics approach. Thousands of presumably healthy people have been found to be suffering early signs of impending emotional disturbances. As victims of an unsuspected mental sickness, they should take steps at once to improve their diet.

To test yourself and see where you stand, we have selected twelve medical-history questions psychiatrists have found to be effective in spotting psychological difficulties. Circle yes or no to each question:

1. Do you have thoughts you can't get out of your head?   yes   no

2. Have you ever felt you were going to have a nervous breakdown? yes no
3. Are you bothered by nervousness and tension? yes no
4. Have there ever been times when you couldn't take care of things because you just couldn't cope? yes no
5. Do you have trouble getting to sleep or staying asleep? yes no
6. Do your hands ever tremble enough to bother you? yes no
7. Are you ever disturbed by nightmares? yes no
8. Are you troubled by your hands sweating? yes no
9. Have you ever fainted or blacked out in recent years? yes no
10. In the past few years have you had headaches? yes no
    If yes, how often?   Every few days   Less often
    Do they bother you?   Quite a bit   Just a little
11. Have you ever had spells of dizziness? yes no
    If yes, how often?   Every few days   Less often
    Do they bother you?   Quite a bit   Just a little
12. Have you ever been bothered by your heart beating hard? yes no
    If yes, how often?   Every few days   Less often
    Does this bother you?   Quite a bit   Just a little

Approximately 78 percent of the adults examined in the National Health Survey were recently reported by the Public Health Service to be experiencing one or more of these symptoms. An average number of "yes" responses for the entire group was 2.29. The conclusion is inescapable: there is a disquieting potential for mental illness simmering in the United States.

Based on such data, we presume that you too have probably circled one or more yes answers. If so, you should take no comfort from the fact that the number of your responses may fall within the "average" range. "Average" cannot be interpreted to mean "healthy."

Any yes response should be taken as a warning. If you have circled two or more yes responses, approaching emotional distress is even more likely. And if, for questions 10, 11, and 12, you circled "every few days" or "quite a bit," we would advise you to seek medical attention.

Early diagnosis can prevent or curb many emotional ailments. The chapters which follow will help. By following the "optimal diet" provided at the end of the book, you should be able to improve dramatically your score on the quiz just completed. (You will also lose weight if you're overweight and gain weight if you're too thin, but this is *not* a diet book. The losing or gaining of pounds will happen because abnormal weight is metabolic in origin.)

The important message is this: you *can* do something about it, whatever "it" is. And that's what *Psychodietetics* is all about.

2

What Causes Emotional Illness: *Is Something Eating You, or Can It Be Something You're Eating?*

On a dreary November day late in 1972, an attractive thirty-six-year-old housewife clutching festively wrapped bundles dragged herself through our office door.

"I can't take it any longer," she burst out. "I set out to do my Christmas shopping today and became so confused and upset that I just gave up. I don't sleep at night, I scream at my children, I argue with my husband. The simplest tasks are overwhelmingly difficult. Worst of all, I feel a complete failure at everything I try to do."

She sat down and continued.

"The other day I was trying to prepare dinner for my family and suddenly discovered I was setting cereal bowls on the table as though it were breakfast. I've even gone to the refrigerator, forgotten what I was looking for, only to discover later that I put the bacon in a kitchen drawer. I feel like I'm losing my mind."

In addition, she told us that she often suffered such serious premenstrual tension that she was virtually inoperative for one week before the onset of her period, that she found it impossible to cope with her responsibilities, was irritable and wracked by attacks of "nerves," headaches, nightmares, an inability to concentrate, and extreme fatigue.

Upon close questioning, she admitted she was at a complete loss to account for any of these emotional disturbances.

"I really have nothing to complain about," she said. "My husband is a good man. We've been married fifteen years and always gotten along well till quite recently. We have a nice home. My three kids are normal, healthy, and active, but I find myself screaming at them for foolish reasons. It's agonizing to see the fear and confusion on their faces when I fly off the handle."

Sixty days later, Mrs. S. was a new woman. The long list of complaints she had presented on her first visit had virtually disappeared. She was composed, relaxed, a woman in control of herself and her life.

Why? What had happened?

Following a complete medical evaluation of Mrs. S., we had quickly recognized the basic cause of her difficulties. She was suffering nutrient deficiencies which complicated and aggravated a metabolic dysfunctioning. Her diet was primarily to blame, for she unerringly chose those foods most likely to upset an already out-of-balance biochemistry. We found that she was addicted to sweets, that she tried to keep going on between-meal snacks that filled her up without nourishing her. *Her emotional state was deteriorating as a result of a combination of nutritionally related metabolic disturbances.*

It is interesting to speculate on the various turns Mrs. S.'s life might have taken had she turned elsewhere for help.

Had she sought conventional medical aid, it is not fanciful to presume that, once a physical examination failed to turn up evidence of organic illness or a specific treatable disease, she would have been told her problems were "all in her mind" and referred to a psychiatrist.

Had she gone to the psychiatrist, it is likely she would still be on the couch, involved in an in-depth exploration of her subconscious mind with an aim toward uncovering early childhood traumas, the presumed psychic damage being rooted in an oppressive upbringing by unresponsive or domineering parents.

Had she joined an encounter group, Mrs. S. and her husband

might be involved in "sensitivity" training sessions with other unhappily marrieds, their sex lives being duly explored while the group leader tried to induce better communication and understanding between them.

Had she joined a Women's Liberation consciousness-raising group, the feminists might have convinced her that she was suffering from a suppressed need for individual fulfillment as she juggled the roles of cook, wife, mother, chauffeur, and handmaiden to a male chauvinist husband.

Had Mrs. S. talked her difficulties over with her mother-in-law, her best friend, her minister, rabbi, or priest, she might have been advised that she needed a vacation, a hobby, a "spiritual retreat," or a "chance to get away from the children."

Had she read any of the popular women's magazines, she might have been convinced that she was suffering the classic symptoms of "tired-housewife syndrome" and have thus been encouraged to try something, anything—from acupuncture to yoga, a trip to a health farm, a face lift, or even an extramarital fling—as a way of relieving her emotional conflicts.

While any of these various therapeutic approaches may hold validity for some people, it is obvious from what actually happened in Mrs. S.'s case that they would all have gone far wide of the mark for her. Some of her problems might have been solved, but she basically would have remained a very unhappy woman.

Our sixty-day "miracle" cure involved no talking out of her problems, no psychotropic drugs to alter her moods or perceptions, no suggestion that she and her husband were approaching the midlife crisis which causes many a marriage to falter in its second decade, and no attempt to convince her that she was merely "acting out" repressed angers and hostilities accumulated during a lifetime.

Our prescription for Mrs. S. included an immediate change to an optimal diet carefully designed to reestablish a proper chemical environment in brain and body cells. In addition, we prescribed a single supplement to be taken at each meal, containing all of the essential and several of the so-called nonessential nutrients. A combination of niacin (vitamin B_3), pyridoxine (vitamin B_6), ascorbic acid (vitamin C), vitamin B_{12}, and d-alpha tocopherol (vitamin E) in megadose quantities was also added to Mrs. S.'s new diet.

In two months, as we have said, a calm and happy woman walked out of our office.

Even if hers were a unique case, it would not be without significance. Doctor W. Shute, a renowned cardiologist and director of the Shute Foundation for Medical Research, recently told one of us: "Even *one* miracle cure shows the efficacy of a novel therapy. One should not have to prove its effectiveness over and over again to gain acceptance."

As matters stand, however, Mrs. S.'s case is *not* unique. Thousands of instances in which nutritional therapy successfully combated a variety of emotional problems rest in our files. These cases are important evidence of the part that diet plays in mental health.

They also bring us to the crucial question of this chapter: what *does* cause mental and emotional illness? Let us study that question before we further explore the prospects for nutritional cures.

To understand why and how the mind sickens, it is necessary to take a brief look at the general history of disease.

In primitive times, both health and disease were considered to be evidence of the capricious nature of the gods. Man believed himself to be cursed by illness when he incurred the wrath of the gods and blessed by health when he pleased them. Thus, his mental condition depended at all times on his relationship with the reigning deities.

As these concepts gradually gave way to the more sophisticated notion that the body's own internal structure was somehow linked with the onset of illness, there followed 2500 years of relentless probing for the underlying cause of disease. As late as the middle 1800s, it was generally accepted that most illnesses resulted from a disturbance in man's internal environment.

In 1865 Louis Pasteur made a discovery from which developed the "germ theory," which has dominated medicine to this day. Once it was known that formerly unheard of microorganisms could invade the body and flourish into specific diseases, the search to seek out, identify, and combat these villains in our environment was underway. It is by no means ended.

The germ theory has suited man's ego quite well. Most of us prefer to believe that the illnesses we suffer are the result of external forces—just as we would rather blame bad luck for our failures. And so we continually say that we "catch" a cold, "get" the flu, and "contract" pneumonia as though we are in no way to blame for the medical catastrophes that befall us.

Germ-theory advocates would have us view man as a helpless quarry eternally trying to elude a multitude of disease-bearing organisms vigilantly intent upon infecting him.

A small cadre of medical practitioners, however, has resisted the germ theory as the one simplistic answer to illness. They have carefully noted that while microorganisms are obviously involved in many ailments, their mere presence does not automatically guarantee disease.

Three healthy people, for example, can breathe the same germs at the same moment. One may develop pneumonia, another may sniffle his way through a cold, and the third may never be aware that the germs were even there. After all, in the case of most infectious diseases, those people who succumb represent only a fraction of the number of people exposed to them.

Is the germ theory obsolete? Certainly more than one noted scientist now espouses a more sophisticated approach to disease. Doctor G. T. Stewart, professor of epidemiology and pathology at the Schools of Public Health and Medicine at the University of North Carolina, points out that polio and other viruses can be carried for months with no effect. "The resulting disease," he says, "is in fact determined by the host, rather than the bacillus."

We are convinced that every disease, physical *and* mental, is generated by a combination of circumstances which arise both inside and outside the body. It logically follows that disease may be prevented or cured by correcting variables that exist both inside and outside the body: *we can go after the "germ," but we can also correct the life condition which predisposed the individual to illness.*

In understanding how emotional illness develops, it is vital that we expand our definition of germs to include those of the psychic variety. "Psychic germs" are often as hard to pin down as the other kind. They come in many forms and degrees, and their ability to infect varies. We normally refer to them as "stresses" or "interpersonal conflicts." Psychiatrists consistently explore their patients' lives for evidence of parental inadequacies, sibling rivalry, repressed sexual desire, suppressed hostility, feelings of inadequacy, and other deep-rooted causes for emotional upset when seeking to cure emotional illness.

Yet, just as a person's body may exhibit lower resistance (higher susceptibility) to the microorganisms that Pasteur first discovered, so does the mind become more vulnerable to emotional distress when it is insufficiently fortified against assaults of a psychic nature.

We all live in a germ-laden atmosphere—physical and psychic germs abound on all sides. Both mind and body can become less susceptible to disease if their resistance to both kinds of germs is increased. Proper diet and nutrition, as we shall demonstrate, are critical to developing that resistance.

Fifty years ago, a new concept of medicine dramatically emphasizing the relationship of mind and body was introduced when the word "psychosomatic" first appeared in German medical literature. Today, that concept is generally accepted.

In *Psychosomatics*, an excellent survey of the literature on the subject by Howard and Martha Lewis, the authors show how emotions can alter endocrine balance, impair blood supply and blood pressure, impede digestion, change body temperature, and produce a sustained state of emotional stress causing physiological changes that lead to disease.

Emotional distress is one *resistance-lowering* factor. Another major factor, according to some health professionals, is the impact of major life changes. Virtually all illness, they believe, is preceded by a constellation of significant events in our lives.

Principal researchers behind this life-change theory of disease are Dr. Thomas Holmes, a professor of psychiatry at the University of Washington, and Dr. Richard H. Rahe, of the United States Navy Medical Neuropsychiatric Unit in San Diego. Rahe is also affiliated with the Department of Psychiatry and the Brain Research Institute at the University of California in Los Angeles.

These doctors, having concluded that mental and physical illness is always preceded by a pattern of significant life changes, believe that future health or disease can be forecast by evaluating these events. The greater the number of life changes, say Holmes and Rahe, the more serious the oncoming illness.

Holmes, Rahe, and their associates devised a numerical system for predicting the chances for succumbing to sickness. They call their diagnostic test the *Social Readjustment Rating Scale*. From thousands of interviews with patients, they selected 43 particularly significant life-change variables. Each patient was requested to rank these events in order of importance. Numerical values were then assigned to each of the 43 life changes, ranging from a low of 11 to a high of 100 points.

Are you ready to gaze into your health future? Then circle yes or no to each life event in this list that has happened to you during the past twelve months.

Life Event	Answer		Point Value
death of spouse	yes	no	100
divorce	yes	no	73
marital separation	yes	no	65
jail term	yes	no	63
death of close family member	yes	no	63
personal injury or illness	yes	no	53
marriage	yes	no	50
fired from work	yes	no	47
marital reconciliation	yes	no	45

Life Event	Answer		Point Value
retirement	yes	no	45
change in family member's health	yes	no	44
pregnancy	yes	no	40
sex difficulties	yes	no	39
addition to family	yes	no	39
business readjustment	yes	no	39
change in financial status	yes	no	38
death of close friend	yes	no	37
change to different line of work	yes	no	36
change in number of marital arguments	yes	no	35
mortgage or loan over $10,000	yes	no	31
foreclosure of mortgage or loan	yes	no	30
change in work responsibilities	yes	no	29
son or daughter leaving home	yes	no	29
trouble with in-laws	yes	no	29
outstanding personal achievement	yes	no	28
spouse begins or stops work	yes	no	26
starting or finishing school	yes	no	26
change in living conditions	yes	no	25
revision of personal habits	yes	no	24
trouble with boss	yes	no	23
change in work hours, conditions	yes	no	20
change in residence	yes	no	20
change in schools	yes	no	20
change in recreational habits	yes	no	19
change in church activities	yes	no	19
change in social activities	yes	no	18
mortgage or loan under $10,000	yes	no	17
change in sleeping habits	yes	no	16
change in number of family gatherings	yes	no	15
change in eating habits	yes	no	15
vacation	yes	no	13
Christmas season	yes	no	12
minor violation of the law	yes	no	11

Now, circle the point value for each yes answer and total the points. According to Holmes and Rahe, you have a 37 percent chance (roughly one out of three) of getting sick within the next two years if your point total is 150 or less. With a total of 151 to 299, assume a 50–50 crack at illness. If the point total is 300 or above, you have an 80 percent chance of becoming ill within the next two years.

Remember, these researchers assert that the higher the score, the more serious the malady. Thus, scores above 300 are believed by them to be predictive of killing and crippling problems like cancer, heart disease, and psychosis.

Yet even a high life-change score may not mean succumbing to disease if one knows how to prevent those stresses and strains from increasing susceptibility or lowering resistance. A vaccination against life changes can, in fact, be achieved in many instances through a strong emphasis on *diet* (the daily intake of food and drink) and *nutrition* (all of the processes involved in using food-stuffs for the body's growth, maintenance, and repair). If you scored high on the life-change test, take heart: your diet can protect you. It can help you maintain your health and your sanity.

The chemical compounds that are found in food act as resistance or susceptibility agents. Some fifty of these substances have been clearly identified to date. Others are strongly suspected in food, but as yet have eluded identification. There are surely others that have completely escaped our attention. It seems reasonable to assume that from 75 to 100 essential nutrients will be discovered before the task of identifying them is complete.

In *Nutrition Against Disease*, Dr. Roger Williams discusses the importance of nutrients in the environmental control of mental disease.

The ... most important way of improving the environment of the brain cells of the [mentally] afflicted or threatened individual is to give them an opportunity of receiving the full nutritional chain of life—not an abbreviated or mutilated version. The brain cells ultimately get from the blood only those nutrient elements that are furnished in the food we eat.

A few years ago, Dr. Linus Pauling published an article in which he highlighted the supremacy of nutrition in correcting abnormalities in the chemical environment of the brain. *Ascorbic acid, thiamin, niacinamide, pyridoxine, vitamin B₁₂, folic acid, magnesium, glutamic acid,* and *tryptophane* were specifically designated as intimately linked to brain function and mental illness.

Of these essential nutrients, vitamin B_3 (niacin or niacinamide) has received the most publicity. If B_3 were the sole nutrient needed for optimal brain cell function, the prevention and treatment of mental illness would be a simple matter indeed. As it is, the brain, like every other organ, requires all of the essential nutrients.

Dr. Williams widens the list to include *riboflavin, pantothenic acid, biotin, iodine, potassium,* all *essential amino acids* (with special emphasis on *lysine* and *threonine*), and *inositol.* For the entire group, these nutrients plus those cited by Professor Pauling, he cites scientific evidence that mental illness is caused primarily by nutritional deficiences in the brain cell environment.

Dr. Williams and other scientists list a variety of emotional conditions stemming from essential nutrient deficiences or improved by nutrient supplementation.

vitamin B_3 deficiency	insomnia, nervousness, irritability, confusion, apprehensiveness, depression, hallucination
thiamin deficiency	loss of appetite, depression, irritability, confusion, memory loss, inability to concentrate, sensitivity to noise
riboflavin deficiency	depression
pantothenic acid deficiency	depression, unable to tolerate stress

pyridoxine deficiency	abnormal responses in psychotic children
vitamin B_{12} deficiency	difficulty in concentration and remembering, stuporous depression, severe agitation, hallucinations, manic or paranoid behavior
biotin deficiency	depression, lassitude, panic, hallucinations
vitamin C administration	improvement in schizophrenia
niacin supplementation	improvement in schizophrenia
iodine deficiency	cretinism
potassium deficiency	nervousness, irritability, mental disorientation
magnesium deficiency	paranoid psychosis
threonine deficiency	irritability, hard to get along with
lysine deficiency	inability to concentrate
glutamic acid administration	improvement in intelligence and general brain functioning in mental retardation
folic acid supplementation	improvement in psychosis
lactate excess in blood	anxiety, neurosis, fatigue, insomnia, tension
calcium deficiency	anxiety, neurosis, fatigue, insomnia, tension

Such a list is reasonable evidence that a host of nutrients affect the chemical milieu of brain cells. Brain cells, in fact, need *every* essential nutrient, and a shortage of any one of them will alter brain function to one degree or another. After all, there is no body activity in which nutrition is not involved; diet does furnish the raw materials or nutrients required for the synthesis of chemical substances indispensable to the body's growth, maintenance, and repair (enzymes, cofactors, hormones, metabolites).

Further, and this point cannot be overemphasized, all nutrients are interrelated. In other words, *the optimal functioning of every single nutrient is dependent upon the presence of every other essential nutrient.*

Doctors Harte and Chow, celebrated researchers in the field of nutrition, reviewed over 200 scientific studies of dietary interrelationships. Their findings reveal that the shortage of a *single* essential vitamin, mineral element, amino acid, or fatty acid will create a shock wave that spreads to affect the utilization and/or function of every other essential nutrient.

Considering how closely related are diet and nutrition to mental health, just how much cause for concern is there over what Mr. and Mrs. America and their children are eating today?

Although we shall cover this subject fully in a later chapter, a sneak preview is in order right now.

Let's take niacin, that nutrient recognized as highly important in the prevention and treatment of mental illness. Being classified as a *resistance agent* (it discourages disease when present and encourages disease when in short supply), niacin gains a plus (+) on our health score card. Now, the Food and Nutrition Board of the National Research Council suggests that male Americans need about 14 to 20 milligrams (a milligram is one thousandth of a gram) of niacin every day, including the niacin formed within the body from one essential amino acid. Yet a recent analysis of male doctors' diets revealed that 12 percent, or one out of eight, were subsisting on less than the *minimal* niacin recommendation.

The proposed niacin recommendation for females ranges from 13 to 16 milligrams per day. Yet 33 percent of the doctors' wives were found to have diets deficient in this important resistance factor.

Is it surprising that one out of every ten adults is a likely prospect for mental illness?

One more sneak preview before this chapter closes. Highly refined or processed carbohydrate foodstuffs contribute little more than calories. Refined carbohydrates are classified as *susceptibility agents* (oversupply encourages disease) and, as such, they are a minus (—) on our health score card. Since refined carbohydrates are grossly lacking in vitamins, minerals, essential fats, and protein, these foodstuffs are quite correctly labeled *empty calories*. This group embraces table sugar, many precooked breakfast cereals, white flour, white (polished) rice, all highly sweetened foods (desserts, sweetened beverages, candy), and both sweetened and unsweetened baked goods made from white wheat flour. It is interesting to note that about one-half of these empty calories are derived from table sugar alone!

Back to the doctors' diets. On the average, about 79 grams of refined carbohydrates were being consumed daily. Since 79 grams is roughly 20 teaspoonfuls, that average intake is almost equal to a teaspoonful per hour around the clock. In fact, some of the doctors and their wives were gobbling up as much as 223 grams of these foodstuffs every day, some 50 teaspoonfuls, a bit over a teaspoonful every 30 minutes!

It is easy to see that these doctors' and their wives' dietary patterns increase their susceptibility to mental disorders. *Your daily diet is probably no better and possibly worse.* To find out, be sure to test its nutritional value by completing the short questionnaire in Chapter 12.

If what you have learned thus far is causing you alarm, let us emphasize that ignorance of these facts should be the greatest reason for concern. Facts can be learned—and, once learned, applied. The pace of today's society, the frantic rules of conduct under which most people live are not conditions that can easily be changed. Yet the food that crosses your plate *can* be changed. Your knife and fork can be your best defensive weapons against illness, whether emotional or physical. *Psychodietetics* offers a battle plan.

3

The Dieting Craze:
It Can Drive You Crazy!

What could be worse than carelessly eating your way into an emotional ailment?

Eating your way into an emotional ailment *deliberately*.

Corrine K., now thirty-five, hasn't been satisfied with the way she looks, or feels, since her first child was born. That was ten years ago.

She had never had a weight problem before becoming pregnant. Then, for almost nine months, she worried over every ounce gained. Her obstetrician believed his mothers-to-be should add as few pounds as possible.

"Monthly checkups were terrible," she remembers. "I didn't even drink water on the day of my appointment, because he'd chew me out for gaining more than a pound or two since my last visit."

Corrine had an easy delivery, and a beautiful son, but she went from her prepregnancy weight of 121 pounds to a post-delivery 135 pounds shortly afterward, and more or less stayed there.

When she came to our office in January 1972 she confessed she'd been on a diet for almost a decade. She was able to shed as much as ten pounds when she really "worked at it," but the weight came back whenever she relaxed and ate "normally."

"I must have lost a hundred pounds in the last few years," she said, "for all the good that's done me."

At 121 pounds, Corrine felt fine, physically and emotionally.

Each time her weight reached 135, the bottom dropped out of her world. Now at her "top weight," she reported, "I can't even wear my contact lenses. My eyes feel fat. Can you believe it?"

She had difficulty getting up in the morning, and once she did it seemed to take her hours to "get started." At night, she would fall asleep easily, exhausted, and then wake up at 3:00 A.M. to toss and turn.

"I can't face living this way the rest of my life," she said. "Jittery, uneasy, restless, muddled . . . . Sometimes I hate my husband. He thinks I'm silly to carry on so about my weight. I know I hate all the doctors who have told me this is all imaginary. And I despise the dieting especially since the pounds always come back."

Corrine has a problem common among women her age: a distorted metabolism triggered by pregnancy. Hormonal changes and metabolic alterations combined so that her former eating habits now caused weight gain. The "lose-ten-pounds-easy" diets she would follow so religiously had only aggravated the metabolic disorder.

We immediately prescribed the Optimal Diet, which not only ended Corrine's up-and-down weight cycle but also did away with the emotional penalty she had been paying. Her nervousness, depression, dizziness, and occasional feelings of panic all disappeared along with the excess weight. Her weight stabilized at 122 pounds, where it is today. She has continued to follow the Optimal Diet, knowing now that her distorted biochemistry was the source of her difficulties all along.

At last count, there were 17,290 methods to reduce weight on public record. And yet, the dieter's chances of finding a safe, effective reducing plan are extremely poor.

Every new weight-reduction proposal makes its debut with messianic fervor. Like a long-awaited savior, the diet-doctor-of-the-month alerts the faithful that the diet-to-end-all-diets has been discovered.

Even the skeptical pounce on a new promise that they can lose weight quickly and with little effort. ("Let's read this while we eat lunch.") The diets reach a huge market, for an estimated seventy-nine million American adults are overweight. More than half of them are struggling to keep their weight down, and at least ten million are actively reducing.

"I wish my wife would lay off the dieting," many a husband has complained. "She turns into such a bitch."

Why the bitchiness? What makes most dieters so nervous? Are the well-recognized "diet doldrums" a psychological reaction to the drudgery of dieting, or do diet-related tensions have a more ominous significance?

Medical experts have repeatedly warned us all of the health hazards risked by indiscriminate dieting: heart disease, arthritis, kidney failure, gall-bladder disorder, even cancer. Yet few professionals have cautioned dieters about the emotional hazards, despite the fact that mental complaints are the *most common* aftermath of dieting.

Those dieters who quip, "I'd rather be *dead* than fat," should reconsider their options. They may inadvertently be choosing between obesity and sanity, especially when they resort to crash dieting.

Israeli researchers who studied ten diet casualties committed to a psychiatric institution discovered that drastic weight reduction has its most shattering effect on the nervous system. Six of the ten dieters had never suffered from emotional problems prior to this *first* attempt at rapid weight loss. There was a direct correlation between the severity of their mental aberrations and the speed, and the amount of weight loss. The better the diet "worked," the sicker the dieter eventually became. The researchers sensibly concluded that there must be a considerable incidence of less serious and therefore unreported emotional disturbances caused by dieting.

Any adult diet allowing an intake of fewer than 2100–2400 calories a day is likely to be deficient in some of the vitamins, minerals, and essential trace elements needed to maintan mental health. Despite the risk inherent in reducing food intake below this caloric level, most reducing regimens advise half that amount.

Whenever food intake is inadequate, the brain, like the body, must draw on reserves to function. During the early stages of deficiency there are generally no signs that this "borrowing" process is taking place. But eventually, depending on the dieter's nutritional bank balance, the reserves are depleted. He grows nervous, is susceptible to suggestion, finds it harder to make decisions, is easily upset; he may even grind his teeth while asleep. Additional dietetic stress can escalate minor emotional symptoms into full-blown neuroses and psychoses.

The brain differs from other organs in its extreme sensitivity. When deprived of oxygen for only a few minutes, it is beyond repair. When essential proteins, fatty acids, vitamins, and minerals are not sufficiently available, brain cells degenerate rapidly. A deteriorating emotional and intellectual state is bound to result.

What happens to the dieter depends in large part on his condition *before* the reducing project is initiated. There is no such thing as being "perfectly healthy but somewhat overweight." In one of our studies we found that subjects only ten pounds overweight had more dandruff, more hemorrhoids, more flat feet, more varicose veins, and more dental decay than those whose weight levels were normal. Their nails and hair did not grow as fast. Most important, they reported more psychological complaints.

A healthy person has a body working in delicate balance; the overweight person does not. Dr. Neil Solomon, Secretary of Health and Mental Hygiene for the State of Maryland, examined more than a thousand obese patients over an eight-year period. He found that *96 percent* showed some inability to digest certain types of foods; 37 percent were not metabolizing glucose properly; 28 percent had difficulty with protein metabolism; 73 percent had fat metabolism problems; and 18 percent had an abnormal basal metabolism—all conditions that are rarely found in the person whose weight is normal.

Dr. Solomon's conclusion is that *not all,* but *many* of the overweight are metabolically abnormal. He believes this condition to be the *result* of their excess poundage, brought about by years of improper eating, rather than the cause. Their metabolism must first be corrected before it will be possible for them to diet, reduce, and regain health.

The overweight person, having been in a less-than-optimal nutritional state for some time, is particularly vulnerable to further impairment of his biochemistry when he's seduced into trying a quick-and-easy diet.

The degree of vulnerability is dramatically illustrated by two studies that evaluated personality changes brought about by putting people who had no need to lose weight on reducing diets. Thirty-six men of normal weight volunteered to participate in an experiment at the University of Minnesota. The evaluators who interviewed them for the project judged the men to be emotionally stable: a "highly idealistic, fun-loving, healthy" group.

For six months they lived on a 1500-calorie diet. None of them became physically ill. *All* of them suffered psychological deterioration. They became weak, irritable, apathetic, and antisocial. Many of them lost interest in women—they were so obsessed with thoughts of food that all other activities ranked second.

A few of the volunteers exhibited such serious disturbances that they had to drop out of the study at the halfway point. The rest suffered lasting psychological scars. They were never quite the same again. Long after the experiment was over, they were still acting like cynical, suspicious neurotics.

A similar study was carried out at the Mayo Clinic by Senior Physician Dr. Russell Wilder. This time the subjects were an emotionally healthy group of young women who had no need to lose weight but volunteered to live together in a clinic under Dr. Wilder's supervision and eat a restricted diet for an extended period of time.

Before three months had passed, the women's personalities underwent startling changes. They began to quarrel endlessly with one another. They experienced unprovoked feelings of anxiety, persecution, and hostility. Some suffered nightmares; others felt extreme panic at times. One woman said she constantly felt as though "something terrible was about to happen." Their memories became faulty; they were clumsy around the work labs and had trouble paying attention to assigned tasks. Dr. Wilder had created a group of "neurotics."

Remember that both experiments used *healthy* people as test subjects. The overweight are *not* healthy and are even more easily upset. Also, the volunteers for these experiments were exposed to only *one* reducing program. Most dieters go on and off such programs sporadically. The pounds, too, go on and off, in an all too familiar pattern Dr. Solomon calls the "yo-yo" syndrome. Each new diet brings new distress.

One psychiatrist who has dealt with the disturbed end products of constant dieting is Dr. Hilde Bruch of the Baylor College of Medicine. Some of her serious cases are described in her book *Eating Disorders*. One thirty-six-year-old man checked in weighing 255 pounds; over a period of twenty years he had lost and regained more than a ton of weight.

His experience is not exceptional. Dr. Bruch also treated a twenty-year-old girl who had managed to lose and regain 530 pounds in the years since her thirteenth birthday. Her eating sprees were followed by rigid reducing. At one point her weight soared to 174; at her lowest, she was an emaciated 77. When she reached the point of complete isolation, cut off from her friends, unable to hold a job, she was admitted to a psychiatric hospital.

Our own experience with thousands of patients shows that approximately 90 percent of all females over the age of thirty, and about half the men, have been on at least one, and more often several, reducing plans at some period in their lives. Those with the most serious complaints are frequently the patients who have dieted most zealously.

Since women are more weight conscious and start dieting at an earlier age, they far outnumber men on reducing-diet casualty lists. Adolescent girls often embark on their first reducing program the same day they creep into a lingerie department for their first brassiere. Preoccupied with appearance and totally unconcerned with health, they begin to worry about "getting fat" at the onset of puberty. Recent estimates indicate that one-fifth of the nation's high-school graduates are overweight by the time they get their diplomas and those who succeed in taking weight off seldom succeed in keeping it off.

The "yo-yo" dieter, whether a teen-ager or an adult, first endangers mental functioning while losing weight, and, again, while gaining it back. Brain cells depend on a *stable* and *complete* supply of nutrients to maintain their equilibrium, just as you depend on a steady income to establish a comfortable life style. If you worked for an irrational boss who sometimes threw an extra fifty bucks in your pay envelope but more frequently held back half your salary with no warning, you would find yourself in a constant financial bind. If it happened too often, you could not remain solvent.

Frequent dieting brings on emotional bankruptcy in much the same manner. Now-you-see-them, now-you-don't nutrient supplies distort the brain's functioning, and the mind grows metabolically frantic.

Few dieters realize how seriously they may be compounding both physical and emotional problems by prolonged dieting. In rare instances, compulsive dieting leads to revulsion toward foods—an inability to eat much of anything. Such ultra-successful dieters come close to starving themselves out of existence, and on occasion even die of malnutrition.

One patient who lived to tell about her experiences confessed that she began dieting because "everybody else at college was doing it." She was a healthy 125 pounds when she began to see how much weight she could lose, "just for fun." At 110 pounds, the game got out of hand. She couldn't stop. She reached 95 pounds with the help of laxatives. At 85 pounds she was living on 400 calories a day, and each day she tried to see if she could eat a little less than the previous day.

By this time she was weak, lethargic, depressed, and suicidal. The psychiatrist called in found it a miracle she was not dead. Her hair had fallen out, her joints were swollen (a form of edema caused by lack of protein), her menstrual cycle had stopped, her thoughts were slowed, and her mind was garbled. She had low blood pressure, hypoglycemia, and could not be forced to take *any* food.

"There are more like me than anyone knows," she said later.

Fanatical dieters who are near the perilous point are to be found in many social settings where it's "in" to be "thin." The highest-paid fashion models consider fainting between assignments to be an occupational hazard, and many middle- and upper-class women with bony but fashionable figures boast they feel stuffed after a lettuce-leaf lunch, never realizing that they have distorted their metabolic process. They have been called "thin fat women"—seen by the world, and often their doctors, as "slender" and therefore "healthy."

Is there any such thing as a *safe* reducing diet? Can you shed excess weight without risking your sanity?

We shall leave to others the task of comparing and debating the values of specific reducing programs. *Rating the Diets*, a Consumer Guide publication, is one available source of impartial information about various popular plans. In it, the Weight Watchers' Diet and program are given "four stars." Weight Watchers offers a sympathetic and homey atmosphere plus group support at their meetings, much like Alcoholics Anonymous. They emphasize a long-term approach and the need to establish new and healthful lifelong eating patterns.

Weight Watchers does not, however, represent *the* solution to the problem of excess weight. Like Alcoholics Anonymous, the success of the Weight Watchers' program is heavily dependent upon the individual's willingness and ability to go along with it. It's more helpful than most programs because it takes nutritional needs into consideration.

A useful rule of thumb is: the "faddier" the diet, the "freakier" the consequences. A diet that "works" by severely limiting varieties of food will live up to its promise: you will lose weight, for a time. You will also lose your serenity. The longer you stay on a diet that places whole categories of foods on a taboo list, the more quickly you approach the danger zone of mental collapse.

One- or two-food diets (like the Grapefruit Diet, the Bananas-and-Milk Diet, the Rice Diet, the Strawberries-and-Cream Diet, the Egg-and-Orange Diet, the Meat-and-Mushroom Diet, and the Pumpkin-Carrot Diet, now sweeping Australia and headed this way) all offer too much of one nutrient, not enough of others. Lopsided diets either aggravate preexisting metabolic imbalances, making them more difficult to correct, or trigger the imbalance where it did not previously exist.

There's a good news–bad news aspect to such diets. The good news: their monotony is apt to bore you into quitting before you suffer too much harm. The bad news: you are likely to shed some weight (how many bananas can anyone eat?) and be encouraged to continue. Determined dieters can Johnny-one-note their way into a mental breakdown.

Several popular diets have as their mainstay a reducing formula in liquid form. These products, it is claimed, supply 100 percent of the body's nutritional needs. The fact is, *no one* has yet gathered the information necessary to compound such a formula. Any number of factors have yet to be isolated and identified. For example, there are antifatigue nutrients, found only in liver and wheat germ oil, so effective that adding either of these food items to the diet of animals who are strenuously exercised prolongs their endurance 300 or more percent. The wheat germ oil nutrient was only recently identified as a vegetable wax called octacosanol. There is also a nutrient factor in carrots that reduces the body's need for oxygen. No one knows what it is or how to refine it. Any one of the many unknown factors may be the very one you need the most. A liquid-diet formula is the last place you'll find it.

Let's look at the low-carbohydrate diets which identify carbohydrates as villains fattening the unwary. These diet plans make the mistake of treating all carbohydrate foods alike, and they're not—by a long shot.

Two slices of ordinary white bread add up to 30 carbohydrate grams, as do two slices of a whole-grain product. Yet the whole-grain bread supplies considerable amounts of thiamin, riboflavin, niacin, vitamin E, and other vitamins and minerals, while the white bread contains hardly any. The 25 carbohydrate grams in two large fresh peaches cannot be equated with the 25 grams to be found in half a cup of canned fruit cocktail: the first supplies almost 3,000 International Units of vitamin A; the second a measly 180.

A legitimate diet should discriminate between constructive and destructive carbohydrate foods. Fruits, vegetables, whole-grain breads and whole-grain cereals are relatively high in carbohydrates, but they are also important sources of hard-to-come-by B vitamins and other essential nutrients. White bread, soda crackers, candy, pastries, and sweet rolls are high in carbohydrates, but these can safely be eliminated: they contain few essential nutrients.

What about the all-protein diets? Can you stay healthy on one of those?

Not for long. Protein foods are the mainstay of life and should be abundantly included in everybody's diet. But even with protein you can have too much of a good thing when other essentials are eliminated. The more protein you consume, the more calcium, magnesium, and other nutrients you must include in your food supply, since their requirements are directly related to protein consumption. High-mineral foods—whole-grain breads and cereals, fresh green vegetables, and peanut butter—are often shunned by carb-counting dieters. Magnesium deficiency, which makes people extremely nervous and distraught, is but one of the unsuspected consequences of rigid dieting.

The diets that limit total calories are the simplest to follow. Armed only with a Bowmar Brain and a calorie guide, you can wend your way through a maze of foods and stop eating at the prescribed cutoff point! Or can you? Low-calorie diets don't work particularly well for most people, but they will probably be with us forever. Most reducing programs, after all, are variations of the "eat less, exercise more" theory, which insists that all weight gain is the result of too much input and too little outgo. Many such diets bill themselves as well-thought-out and nutritionally superb plans. We have chosen one such well-meaning diet to analyze—not the best or the worst, just typical.

In the March 1973 issue of *Good Housekeeping* there appeared a 1200-calorie reducing program designed to be part of a "Shape Up Now" seven-day schedule. The menu plan advised prospective dieters to choose foods from the "Basic-Four Food Families," including two servings daily of meat, four of vegetables or fruits, four of bread, and two of milk. One "meat" serving might consist of 3 ounces of lean cooked meat, fish, or poultry, or 2/3 cup of tuna. If an egg or 1/2 cup of cottage cheese was chosen for breakfast, the meat at lunchtime was to be cut to 2 ounces.

According to this diet plan, a fruit or vegetable serving equals 1/2 cup of canned or cooked fruit, 1 fresh apple or peach; 1/2 banana; 1/2 cup cooked vegetables; 1 small ear of corn; or 1 cup greens.

The "bread-cereal" serving was to be selected from the following: 1 slice of any bread, 1 small roll, a breadstick, 1/2 cup of potatoes, pasta, rice, or cooked cereal, 4 saltines, Melba toast, or graham crackers, 1 cup ready-to-eat cereal, 1 biscuit or muffin.

The milk serving could be 1 cup of skimmed milk, buttermilk, or plain yogurt.

Specific menu plans for each of the seven days were included. These must have been chosen with an eye toward making the reducing plan "adventurous"; there is no *nutritional* excuse for suggesting "Breakfast Number Five": green pea soup, saltine crackers, and milk.

On the same day lunch was more traditional fare: cottage cheese, fresh fruit platter on romaine lettuce, Melba rounds, and milk. Dinner verged on the daring: ham steak, sweet potato, green beans, biscuit with jelly, and "lime Bavarian" for dessert.

If the dieter conscientiously followed the plan, on the fifth day she might be feeling virtuously hungry. If she was also beginning to feel tired, irritable, and hard to live with, that's understandable, since she was getting only about half the essential nutrients needed to maintain emotional well-being.

Depending on the specific foods chosen this day, she was getting either a smattering of vitamin C or virtually none. There was a nutritional difference if she chose fresh green beans for dinner rather than canned. The diet left it up to the reader, as though the way a food is processed made no difference in its food value.

You simply cannot treat vitamin needs like choices on a menu in a Chinese restaurant: take two from Column A and one from Column B and trust to luck that the combination will work out.

Four of the suggested menu plans also violate a very basic tenet of good nutrition: the absolute necessity of beginning the day with a variety of foods that get the metabolic process in motion with an ample supply of all essentials: citrus fruits, whole grains, and whole protein in the form of eggs or meat. A proper breakfast should provide at least 1/3 of the daily total calorie and protein needs.

Summed up, this diet plan—although undoubtedly well intentioned—makes the same nutritional errors common to most similar weight-loss diets. The emphasis on a restricted number of total calories suggests weight gain or loss is exclusively dependent upon caloric intake.

The 1200 calories per day allowance seriously limits the intake of vitamins, minerals, essential fats and protein, and cannot provide for an optimal supply of these essential nutrients.

The diet ignores the great difference between refined carbohydrates (incomplete calories containing little or no protein, vitamins, minerals, and essential fatty acids) and unrefined carbohydrates (completed calories in terms of essential nutrient content).

The diet plan makes no provision for completing nutrient needs through nutritional supplementation. In other words, it is yet another semi-starvation regime.

Many of the foods recommended in the seven-day menu plan are loaded with nutritionally depleted or empty calories—raspberry applesauce, white bread, canned fruits, noodles, graham crackers, vanilla wafers, sugar-coated cornflakes, saltines, biscuits, lime Bavarian, jelly rolls, muffins, and white rice.

Seven days of such an eating program does not, of course, guarantee emotional disaster. But seven days followed by seven more, and then another seven, *will* deplete brain cells—with the result that emotional problems become obvious long before the dieter has managed to get into a size 10 bathing suit. Dr. Bruch has described such seven-times-seven dieters as chronically depressed, fearful of desertion and loneliness, and metabolically out of control. Long-term therapeutic programs are required to correct all of their diet-caused deficiencies.

Frequently the patient is the last to realize that her difficulties are in any way related to her reducing efforts.

"Isn't it healthy to stay thin? What's dieting got to do with the way I feel?" a typically uninformed victim asked when we took her case history.

An emotional wreck at the age of twenty-nine, Mrs. M. was in the throes of her second divorce. Her most recent husband had walked out, she claimed, because she was a sloppy housekeeper.

"The house was a mess," she admitted, "but I'm so exhausted most of the time, I don't see why I should be blamed for that."

Mrs. M. pointed out that she took great pride in her appearance. Any reasonable man, she told us, should appreciate having a wife who kept herself slim and attractive, especially after mothering two children.

"It's always been a struggle," she said. "I've had to count every calorie since I was a kid. If I go off my diet even for a minute, I'll get fat."

She was proud of her will power: "I'm often *really* hungry, but I rarely give in to myself."

It wasn't easy to convince this patient that her depression, exhaustion, headaches, and anxieties all stemmed from chronic malnutrition—that she was on the verge of collapse because of nutrient depletion. After the results of her medical tests were analyzed and explained, she agreed to try a corrective diet with nutrient supplementation.

Within six months, she said, "I'm feeling great. No depression, no exhaustion. The world has become a nicer place, and I know I'm a nicer person." Her fear of getting "fat" had not materialized, and her reconciliation with her husband made up for needing a one-size-larger wardrobe.

Could your own problems have been triggered by attempts to lose weight? Are you a potential diet disaster? Answer the following questions by circling either Yes or No.

1. Have you been on two or more reducing diets during the past five years?   yes   no
2. Has your weight fluctuated more than ten pounds, either way, in the past two years?   yes   no
3. Have you ever been on a crash diet?   yes   no
   For more than one week?   yes   no
4. Do you ever try to keep your weight down by skipping meals?   yes   no
5. Do you often have *strong* food cravings?   yes   no
6. Do you gain weight when you are "not dieting"?   yes   no
7. When you stop a reducing diet, do you gain back the weight you lost?   yes   no
8. On your favorite reducing diet, do you lose more than 1½ pounds per week?   yes   no
9. Does your diet seriously restrict and limit the *kinds* of foods you can eat?   yes   no
10. Have you ever restricted your food intake without adding a vitamin-mineral supplement?   yes   no
11. Have you ever taken reducing pills or appetite suppressants to help you lose weight?   yes   no
12. Does your overweight problem date back ten years or longer?   yes   no

Add up your yes answers. If you circled yes three times or more, the chances are that you have suffered some degree of metabolic distortion. If you answered questions 3, 11, or 12 in the affirmative, the possibility that you are biochemically out of balance multiplies.

A sneak preview of the Optimal Diet, found in the final chapter of this book, should be helpful at this point. It is not designed as a reducing diet. It offers no day-by-day menu plans, since it is designed for people, not robots. It is meant to be a lifetime guide to good eating habits, not a "stick-to-this-for-a-week" program that may be followed by a "go-on-a-binge" respite.

The Optimal Diet helps restore your metabolic balance. Since a disturbed metabolism is the underlying cause of both underweight and overweight problems, adherance to the Optimal Diet brings an unexpected bonus: your weight will readjust to a more normal level, up or down, as the case may be. It thins "fatties" and fattens "skinnies."

Here's another fringe benefit: you may learn *for the first time* what your best weight should be. Many a woman who has tried for years to fit into size 10 clothes rightfully belongs in a size 12. The height-weight charts that set out "ideal" weights for "average" people tell you nothing about *you*.

How will you know when you've reached your best weight? Your weight will stabilize, as will your emotions.

The Optimal Diet is a "feel good" diet. It tells you the foods you can eat liberally, because they provide the most nutrition per bite, and those to eat sparingly, particularly if you are overweight. It tells you which foods *everyone* should avoid because they aggravate emotional disturbances almost universally.

Moreover, the Optimal Diet allows the widest variety of food choices. And after a few weeks you will not have to exercise great will power, nor will you feel deprived. Your tastes will readjust in time, so that the "avoid" foods you may now crave will no longer tempt you.

Our patients have found they can't fool us. Occasionally one will confess to having gone on a binge, eating foods discouraged or prohibited by the Optimal Diet. If the patient says, "But I've been on your Optimal Diet most of the time, really," we ask the key question: "Did those forbidden foods taste good?"

Any patient who tells us they *did* is almost certainly fibbing. Adherance to the Optimal Diet for any length of time makes sweet and starchy foods seem unappealing.

Diet "jitters" may seem a small price to pay for a slim figure, but many people who first experienced an "attack of nerves" while on a reducing diet later become much sicker.

You may never have considered emotional disorders as serious as alcoholism, schizophrenia, anxiety neurosis, suicidal depression to be a culmination of nutritional neglect. Think again. "Diet" is a word with ominous overtones. You can "diet" your way into disaster, or you can "diet" yourself into optimal physical *and* mental health. You make the choice.

4

Alcoholism: A "Social" Disease
—Fact or Fancy?

Is alcoholism a "social" disease?

Call an ex-alcoholic "reformed" at your own risk. No *moral* issue has been resolved when a drinker has been cured of his disease.

Mercedes McCambridge is one of many well-known personalities who are "out-of-the-closet" former alcoholics pleading for better public understanding of America's number-one drug addiction—and least understood ailment.

Her message, a simple one, is delivered, with all the fire and guts she can muster: "Alcoholics aren't evil, weak-willed, immoral. I know, because I've been one. Alcoholism isn't a 'social' disease. It's some kind of disaster."

But what kind? Is alcoholism a psychological ailment?

While many authorities now agree that there is no single cause for habitual drinking, emphasis has commonly been placed on family relationships. If there has been mental illness in the family background,—or criminality, neurosis, serious parental discord, divorce, alcoholism, your chances of becoming an alcoholic multiply.

One theory suggests that people who come from unstable backgrounds turn to the bottle in time of need, while those with solid, supportive families turn to friends and relatives. Dr. E. M. Abrahamson, the author of *Body, Mind and Sugar*, takes issue with the "flight-from-reality" hypothesis which has given therapists such a wide arena in which to spar with supposedly villainous parents:

The alcoholic thus is seen as running away from life because he was a rejected child. He had a neurosis, a personality disturbance resulting from the fact that his beloved had jilted him, or married him and shattered his illusions about her. Or he wanted to be a poet or an artist and had been forced by his father into the insurance business. He had wanted to be a composer; he had been forced to become a salesman. So he drank to hear the music he no longer heard at any other time. Et cetera, et cetera, ad infinitum.

Dr. Abrahamson, who clearly does not embrace such theories, would not deny that psychological influences can work to *help* create the alcoholic. And yet, they actually *explain* nothing. Why? Because they are not explanations. They are simply descriptions of the state of affairs that exists in the alcoholic's life.

What kind of an ailment, then, *is* alcoholism?

A great many researchers who have lifted the alcoholic off the couch and placed him under the microscope are convinced that uncontrolled drinking is a metabolic disorder that can be treated by nutritional therapy.

Dr. Roger Williams pulls no punches when he categorically states that no one who follows good nutritional practices ever becomes an alcoholic. In *Nutrition Against Disease*, he backs up this contention: "The fact that some individuals become alcoholics . . . and others, under similar circumstances, do not, is inescapable and is of the utmost importance in understanding the disease."

Doctors are, of course, aware of the fact that alcoholics frequently suffer from malnutrition. But, as Dr. Williams points out, they assume the malnutrition to be the result of the alcoholism, not a contributing factor. Malnutrition of the brain cells is simply not considered as a *cause* of alcoholism.

Dr. Williams has moved beyond theory: he has proved that the wrong diet can *create* an alcoholic. Using the rat for testing, Williams and his colleagues have shown that diets deficient in essential nutrients encourage alcohol consumption in animals, and that their drinking habits can be reversed by adding the missing nutrients to their food.

This research was duplicated at Loma Linda University in California by investigators who induced a craving for alcohol in rats by feeding them a diet high in refined carbohydrates, low in vitamins, minerals, and proteins.

The rats were not psychologically stressed; they were not raised by "mean parents," but they turned eagerly to drink when deprived of proper diet.

Thirty rats were divided into three groups for a sixteen-week study. One group remained on the high-carbohydrate diet; another group ate the same diet supplemented with vitamins and minerals; and a third group consumed a balanced human diet.

The result?

Given a choice between plain drinking water and a 10 percent solution of ethyl alcohol, the rats on the high-carbohydrate diet drank, on an average, fifty milliliters—the equivalent of what would be a quart of 100-proof whiskey a day for an adult man. The rats on the fortified high carbohydrate diet drank only one-third as much alcohol, while those on the well-balanced human diet generally preferred plain water.

Dietary manipulation can turn teetotalers into alcoholics. Twenty percent of a group of rats maintained on the high-carbohydrate diet for five weeks did not develop a taste for alcohol until sugar was added to the solution. These rats then turned into the heaviest drinkers of all. When switched onto a balanced diet, they gradually became *ex*alcoholics.

A Loma Linda University group headed by Dr. U. D. Register conducted a study to determine whether a typical "teen-age diet," known to be nutritionally *marginal* rather than totally deficient, could also cause a craving for alcohol in rats.

Each rat was allowed the choice of drinking a solution composed of 10 percent alcohol and 90 percent water or simply plain water. Their basic diet consisted of glazed doughnuts, sweetened soft rolls, hot dogs, carbonated beverages, spaghetti and meatballs, apple pie and chocolate cake, white bread, green beans, tossed salad, candy, and cookies.

This diet, which might sound disturbingly familiar to many a parent, is marginally deficient in protein, vitamin A, thiamin, riboflavin, niacin, vitamin C, iron, and calcium. Vitally needed trace minerals and lesser-known nutrients are also substandard.

The control diet contained adequate levels of all nutrients as compared with recommended intakes for adolescents. It was composed of vegetables, fruits, nuts, legumes, whole wheat flour, cottonseed oil, sugar, and whole-milk powder.

Rats fed the control diet maintained a low intake level of alcohol. Those fed the marginal teen-age diet tippled freely. They drank even more when coffee or caffeine was added to the teen-age diet. Adding a vitamin supplement greatly reduced alcohol intake.

The heaviest drinkers among the rats could be switched in and out of their alcoholic behavior by a change in diet.

Experiments like these reinforce the idea of a metabolic control mechanism, sensitive to dietary factors, that creates a *biologic thirst* for alcohol. They also offer some rationale for the ever-rising alcohol problem that educators have decried among high school and college students.

The diets described in these experiments might seem quite normal to those who are not aware that heavy consumption of refined carbohydrates creates a dramatic fluctuation in blood-sugar levels. Such disturbances in sugar metabolism cause a condition known as functional hypoglycemia, or low blood sugar. It exists in 70 to 90 percent of alcoholics, seriously impairing their physical and emotional stability and hampering their recovery.

Abnormal sugar metabolism, which may simmer for many years before the drinking problem develops, results, in part, from too much insulin, which is secreted by the pancreas in response to a rapid rise in the circulating blood-sugar level. The abrupt rise occurs following the consumption of table sugar and foods or drinks high in sugar or other refined carbohydrates. The caffeine in medicines, coffee, chocolate, and cola beverages, along with the nicotine from tobacco, also contributes to functional hypoglycemia.

Although alcohol by itself does not directly stimulate insulin release, an abnormally large amount of insulin will be released if the intake of alcohol is followed by an intake of refined carbohydrates. This process might best be described as a priming effect on the pancreas.

Exalcoholics often report that periods of low blood sugar cause a thirst or craving for alcohol, caffeine, nicotine, or sweets. In a great many cases, recovery has quickly followed the correction of a hypoglycemic condition.

Others are not so fortunate. Somber statistics released in 1972 by the National Institute of Alcohol Abuse and Alcoholism revealed that there are more than ninety-five million drinkers in the United States and some nine million alcoholics. Recovery rates are generally low and discouraging, possibly because so much therapeutic emphasis has been placed on psychological factors while the more basic problems, dietary deficiencies and defects in body chemistry, have received relatively little attention.

Frustrated therapists have sometimes resorted to "Clockwork Orange" attempts to shock alcoholics into sobriety.

In a state hospital near Munich, Germany, two California psychologists recruited sixty-eight male volunteers, all of whom were lower-class inveterate drunks, for a typical punishment-oriented experiment. They plied their subjects with liquor for almost two weeks. Then, as their subjects drank, they got intermittent nasty shocks from a 1.5 volt battery along with their booze. After twelve days of this drink-plus-shock regime, none of the men could even smell liquor without choking and gasping. Yet six months later 53 percent of the group had gone back to the bottle.

It is not surprising that pain-laden rehabilitative programs are often ineffective. The built-in "pain" suffered by alcoholics—strained and broken relations with loved ones; loss of prestige, career, income, status, and hope—seldom provides sufficient motivation for drinkers to give up their habits.

Nor can drinkers be frightened by the dangers they face. Public service campaigns aimed at drinking drivers have proved so ineffective that the Honda Motor Company is experimenting with ways in which the car itself may soon police the highways. Honda is developing a sensor that sniffs out a motorist's whiskey breath, then locks the ignition. If the driver cagily starts the engine when he is sober and then begins to drink while driving, the sensor will issue a curt warning to pull over before the motor cuts itself off.

America's number-one health problem has the distinction of being the one ailment that the medical community has largely turned over to the lay public. Doctors, and police officials, family counselors, and social workers, routinely refer excessive drinkers to Alcoholics Anonymous. Although the success of A.A. is impressive, A.A. is not the whole and only answer to alcoholism. Its promise of recovery through the famous Twelve Steps is only to those who are willing to take the *first step*, who will admit they are powerless over alcohol and that their lives have become unmanageable. Unfortunately very few alcoholics take this step.

Dr. Harold Greenwald, a well-known clinical psychologist and author of *Decision Therapy*, has commented that somewhere along the line, for a variety of reasons, the alcoholic has consciously or unconsciously made the "decision" to drink. "Most alcoholics' decisions to stop drinking," he states, "are 'wishes,' not decisions. Often you have to change the chemical composition of a disturbed person with diet or drugs."

Alcoholics and schizophrenics are biochemical kissing kin. In extreme cases their hallucinations are remarkably alike and have similar chemical origins. Common to both are abnormal carbohydrate metabolism, hormone imbalance, nutrient deficiency, liver dysfunction, wheat-grain allergy, and functional or metabolic disorder in the brain.

Of the numerous rehabilitative programs advocated by experts, clinicians have found nutritional therapy to work best. *Megavitamin* therapy, which successfully salvages some schizophrenics, has proved to be dramatically effective with alcoholics.

In an ongoing study of niacin (vitamin B_3) therapy undertaken by Dr. Russell F. Smith, medical director of Michigan State Boys' Training School, 86 percent of the hard-core alcoholics were helped. Niacin doses ranged from 4 to 20 grams, according to need, with an average dose of 6 grams, divided into four doses after meals and at bedtime.

According to Dr. Smith's progress report, his patients were all previously long-time treatment failures, with histories that included every type of therapy. They were "revolving-door drunks." His results, when compared with those of other programs, showed the niacin therapy to be far more effective—especially when you consider the fact that many of the drugs used in other treatments of alcoholism have a high potential for abuse and for suicide.

Among Dr. Smith's successes was a college instructor in English who, on a daily dose of 12 grams of niacin, successfully completed his first full term of teaching in five years. A similar treatment program made it possible for a forty-year-old painter who had both a schizoid background and a drinking history dating back to the age of eleven to remain sober for seven straight months, his longest period of sobriety since childhood.

In a follow-up on the 507 original patients, only 70 were lost either through death or insobriety. The fact that only three were victims of cardiac arrest indicates that niacin also has a beneficial effect on the heart. Long-time alcoholics are extremely high-risk prospects for heart disease.

Well over five thousand alcoholics in all stages of the disease have been added to the study, including several hundred adolescents with acute toxic and chronic organic brain syndromes. These patients have shown improved sleep patterns, reduced anxiety levels, mood stabilization, better coping abilities, occasional dramatic improvement in judgment and memory, sustained job performance, and improved family life.

There were also physical benefits such as reduced withdrawal symptoms, fewer "dry drunks" (shakes and sweats when sober), decreased likelihood of heart attacks and strokes, reduced cholesterol, and lowered blood pressure.

Dr. Smith's program requires no great test of will power. His patients have been able to remain sober with little psychological distress. They have been able to give up psychotropic drugs and voluntarily avoid risking exposure to situations that tend to encourage more drinking.

The B_3 therapy does *not* permit the true alcoholic to return to moderate drinking. It *does* help to prevent relapse into alcoholism. Dr. Smith is convinced that nicotinic acid, one form of B_3, provides an opportunity of striking at the heart of the physiological mechanisms underlying alcohol tolerance, withdrawal, and perhaps even the alcoholic disease process. Its apparent mode of action does not really fit the traditional concepts of a vitamin but rather that of a hormone. In any event, it seems to make a significant difference in the ability to obtain and maintain alcohol abstinence.

Additional confirmation of the megavitamin approach to the treatment of alcoholism comes from the North Nassau Mental Health Center and its director, Dr. David R. Hawkins, who has reported that most of the 600 alcoholics he has treated since 1966 are now fully recovered. In his program patients are given one gram of vitamin B_3, one gram of ascorbic acid, 200 International Units of Vitamin E, all four times a day, and 50 milligrams of pyridoxine once a day. They are also put on a hypoglycemic diet to correct low-blood-sugar problems.

With a success rate of 71 percent, Dr. Hawkins has good reason to crow. Many of his patients were schizophrenic as well as alcoholic and almost all had had previous treatment or hospitalization, some for as long as twelve years. Psychotherapy or psychoanalysis for periods ranging up to twenty years, also common among them, had proved ineffective.

The megavitamin approach for alcoholics is in use by several hundred doctors in the United States and Canada at present, and various aspects of its treatment are under serious research in many parts of the world. The Shadel Hospital in Seattle, Washington, has been treating alcoholism since 1940 by giving patients a vitamin B_3 enzyme, nicotinamide adenine dinucleotide (NAD), to aid recovery, and over the past three decades 66 percent of some fourteen thousand patients have remained totally abstinent after the very first treatment.

Dr. Frank Butler force-feeds his hospitalized alcoholics by inserting a tube in their stomachs through which he can provide a high-protein liquid substance that contains all the known vitamins and essential minerals. He has found that the alcoholic, whose diet does not provide essential nutrients, futilely tries to quiet his quivering nerves and raise his sagging self-confidence by drinking more alcohol. The more he drinks, the more badly nourished he becomes, since alcohol contains nothing but calories.

At Tucson's Veterans Administration Hospital, experimenters are working on a "stay sober" pill for partygoers that has vitamins as its base. They have found, by tests on rats, that injections of vitamin B_3 and vitamin B_6 reduce intoxication time by lowering alcohol levels in the blood and by speeding up the body's use of the substance.

Swedish physicians have also found that a dose of vitamins before drinking alcoholic beverages causes the drinker to feel less drunk.

Dr. Leonard Goldberg, a California researcher, used policemen in his test. Half of them received large injections of vitamin B complex while the balance were injected with fluids containing nothing of value. All of them were then given copious amounts of alcohol to drink. Those who had received the vitamin B shots reported feeling less intoxicated and tested higher on perception and mental acuity tests than their colleagues who had received the placebo.

The nutritional intervention that is licking alcoholism is encouraging and offers possibilities for self-help. The multiple deficiencies of vitamins and minerals created by alcohol dependency are readily reversed by the combination of optimal diet and therapeutic quantities of nutritional supplements, which should be taken with each meal. Besides eating nutritious foods the alcoholic, or near-alcoholic, should stay away from substances that contain caffeine: coffee, certain medications, cola beverages, strong tea, and chocolate. Caffeine and nicotine significantly impair recovery from alcoholism. They not only contribute to hypoglycemia but also produce a further dependency state. In addition, nicotine prevents the body's absorption of vitamin C, a deficiency of which hampers rehabilitation.

One of the most frustrating characteristics of alcoholism is the inability of most drinkers, at *any* stage of the illness, to recognize or accept the fact that their drinking has become a "problem."

Are you willing to face up to the possibility that you may be on the road to alcoholism? Dr. Robert V. Seliger of Johns Hopkins University has developed a series of questions that will help you determine where you stand.

1. Have you lost time from work due to drinking?	yes	no
2. Has drinking made your home life unhappy?	yes	no
3. Do you drink because you are shy with people?	yes	no
4. Has drinking affected your reputation?	yes	no
5. Have you gotten into financial difficulties because of your drinking?	yes	no
6. Do you turn to lower companions and an inferior environment when drinking?	yes	no
7. Does your drinking make you careless of your family's welfare?	yes	no
8. Has your drinking decreased your ambition?	yes	no
9. Do you want a drink "the morning after"?	yes	no
10. Does your drinking cause you to have difficulty sleeping?	yes	no
11. Has your efficiency decreased since drinking?	yes	no
12. Has drinking ever jeopardized your job or business?	yes	no

13. Do you drink to escape from worries or business?   yes   no
14. Do you drink alone?   yes   no
15. Have you ever had a complete loss of memory as a result of drinking?   yes   no
16. Has your physician ever treated you for drinking?   yes   no
17. Do you drink to build up self-confidence?   yes   no
18. Have you ever been in an institution or hospital on account of drinking?   yes   no
19. Have you ever felt remorse after drinking?   yes   no
20. Do you crave a drink at a definite time daily?   yes   no

If you have answered yes to as few as *three* questions, it means that alcohol has become, or is becoming, a serious problem in your life. Although this questionnaire approach suffers the inherent weakness common to any self-appraisal procedure, it has nevertheless proved to be a useful diagnostic tool. Take it seriously.

If alcoholism is suspected or confirmed, it would be wise to have a doctor test immediately for hypoglycemia. A five- or six-hour glucose-tolerance test (seven blood samples) with 100 grams of glucose should be requested.

If a diary is kept during the test, it will be obvious to the patient that many of his or her aggravating complaints are related to changes in the blood-sugar level. Craving for caffeine, nicotine, sugar, or alcohol may occur during or after the test.

Even if you passed the "drinking habits" test with flying colors, remember that poor *eating* habits can make you susceptible to alcoholism whenever you face unusual or heavy psychological pressures. A simple nutritional rule to prevent alcoholism from ever developing has been set forth by Dr. Williams: "It is this—that no more than 10 percent of the calories one consumes day by day be naked or empty calories. If 90 percent of the calories one consumes are in the form of wholesome food, malnutrition will not become a part of life; individuals will never pass through a period of preparation for drinking, which is the prerequisite of becoming an alcoholic."

Anyone who has been on and off the alcoholic merry-go-round himself or with some relative or close friend may find our relatively simple remedies hard to believe, but skeptics-turned-believers are easy to find.

One case is that of a man who, as an A.A. member, had managed to remain sober for many years but was constantly besieged with fits of depression. His life, with or without alcohol, was a continuous struggle. At the suggestion of a friend, he began taking 3000 milligrams a day of niacin and a comparable amount of vitamin C. He noticed almost at once that his energy level increased, he became more emotionally stable, and his bouts of depression and anxiety nearly vanished. His relationships at work and at home improved considerably.

Pleased but still skeptical, he continued his massive vitamin doses for about three years and then just ran out and didn't bother to replenish his supply. "It was just carelessness on my part," he reported, "but within a few weeks, all of my old depression, fatigue, and anxiety came flooding back. As soon as I figured out what was happening, I got more vitamins and my condition very soon improved again. I've become a believer from my own experiences as well as the experience of friends of mine."

Thirty-one-year-old Sharon J., housewife and mother, was still luckier. She secretly feared encroaching alcoholism, although she had never admitted it to anyone. Where once she had enjoyed an occasional cocktail when dining with friends, she now found herself craving a drink at the end of a hectic day—and not always stopping with one. When she couldn't sleep at night, she'd pour herself a drink, "to relax."

"I can always just stop," she'd tell herself. But she didn't. She was afraid that stopping would reveal the extent of her dependency on alcohol.

Sharon came in for her annual checkup, and started talking

about "this friend of mine" who thinks "maybe she has a drinking problem." How could she help her friend?

We went along with the pretense, and explained that vitamin supplements and the Optimal Diet could keep her friend from coming to the feared end. Sharon took the diet and left the office quickly.

Months later, she returned and confessed that she was the "friend."

"The change in eating habits and the vitamins," she said, "leveled me out, made life seem much easier. I no longer think of grabbing a drink when the going gets rough. I have a lot more energy. For the first time in years, I'm sleeping well—and really enjoying myself when I'm awake."

If you have found alcohol a problem in your life, or if your score on the drinking-habits test indicates that a problem is developing, there is a good possibility that all that stands between you and emotional well-being are a change in diet and a few inexpensive vitamin pills each day. In the past decade, many thousands have started life anew on such programs. The fact that there exists such remarkable new hope for alcoholics should end much of the frustration that has surrounded their "incurable" disease.

5

Schizophrenia Is a
Mental Disease: Fact or Fancy?

She began acting strangely right after college graduation.

An attractive, intelligent young woman, she was now confused, moody, depressed, "not herself."

Her troubled family watched and waited, then consulted a psychiatrist, who diagnosed schizophrenia.

For the next five years she was taken from hospital to hospital, treated with everything from tranquilizers to shock therapy.

She got worse.

When her parents heard of a psychiatrist who had successfully treated similar cases by viewing them as metabolic conditions, they turned to him. He tested his patient and found that her mental symptoms were the result of chronic pellagra, a nutritional disease.

Only then did her parents learn that in her senior year their daughter had been on a crash diet, with the help of amphetamines prescribed by a doctor. She had curtailed her food intake so sharply that her body was depleted of essential nutrients, particularly niacin.

She was placed on a carefully supervised diet fortified with heavy doses of vitamin C, niacin, and other B-complex vitamins. Her pellagra gradually disappeared, along with her schizoid symptoms.

This girl's case points up the widely divergent views held by professionals on the cause and treatment of schizophrenia and other "mental" ailments.

Freud, when he first formulated his psychoanalytic theories, had never heard of hormones, enzymes, vitamins; yet he himself believed schizophrenia to be chemical in origin and predicted that it would one day yield to a chemical cure, and he was right.

Biochemistry, although a relatively new discipline, has produced a wealth of discoveries in the past few decades, adding immeasurably to our understanding of human behavior; yet much of this information is ignored by orthodox psychiatrists, who prefer to adhere to pre-1930 concepts.

The majority of psychologically oriented and trained therapists feel threatened by this new approach to mental illness. Like archaeologists, they continue to sift and dig for artifacts, in their case, for destructive psychological factors in a patient's life experiences. The patient may be subjected to any number of therapies, from psychoanalysis to brain surgery.

With what chance for cure?

Estimates of recovery rates from all well-established treatments range from 18 to 40 percent. Some who have recovered resume normal lives; others suffer chronic recurring attacks. About one-third of all diagnosed schizophrenics stumble through life, not sick enough to be institutionalized, not well enough to live a happy, normal life. Another third end up totally disabled, relegated to the back wards of "caretaker" institutions.

Schizophrenia is not a rare ailment. It affects one of every hundred persons in all societies, in all cultures, in all racial and ethnic groups, in all social classes, in times of peace or war, depression or prosperity.

It can strike at any age. Babies can be born with it; college students are frequently afflicted; and it can creep up gradually in the middle years or beyond.

What is schizophrenia like?

The schizophrenic literally "loses his senses." Smells, tastes, sounds, sights, and textures are distorted.

A typical case has been described by L. Galston:

Her name here can be Joan. She lives in a world that sometimes becomes agonizing, even terrifying. There are moments when she hears strange voices, sees haunting shapes. Recurrently the black moods of depression descend upon her and often then at night she is shaken by fits of irrational crying. Sometimes, without warning, moods of sudden fury appear, and, full of fear that she is losing control of herself, it is all she can do not to smash her TV set or a chair or a shelf of dishes. Yet much of the time she manages on the surface to appear self-possessed—though strange. Strange because she is so withdrawn, keeps so much to herself. She has a job, maintains a small apartment, comes and goes quietly, and says hello if a neighbor says it first. At twenty-five she is unmarried. She was once engaged, but nothing came of that. She isn't sure why. Nor does she know why she is totally unable to relate to other people, why her world so often is such an explosive, tormenting one. She has consulted doctors about her headaches, sleeping difficulties, fatigue. But she hasn't mentioned the other troubles. Apprised of them all, given the complete picture, a doctor could have suspected what is really wrong. For Joan is a victim of schizophrenia.

Such bizarre behavior has spawned a vast mythology. The American Schizophrenia Association, devoted to demystifying the condition, explains that it is *not* a way of life, *not* a crime, *not* a "split" personality, *not* a sign of latent homosexuality. In its most informative booklet, *What You Should Know About Schizophrenia*, we find a clear picture of the perceptual changes and personality alterations most frequently experienced. Among them are:

Visual changes: illusions and hallucinations; people and objects appear distorted, as though reflected by a mirror at a sideshow; the real and the unreal blend.

Auditory changes: buzzings, hissings, unseen voices; a whisper can be deafening, a shout not heard.

Changes in sense of smell: pungent aromas fade; perfume may be malodorous, body odors offensive.

Changes in sense of touch: crawling, creepy sensations; a slight touch can be painful, a body blow not felt at all.

Taste changes: familiar foods become strange; poisons are suspected in once-loved foods.

Time changes: the clock stops, then races; past, present, and future are confusingly intertwined.

Changes in thought process: memory is disturbed; logic suspended; the mind speeds or slows without reason.

Changes in thought content: Napoleonic-type complexes; delusions of personal power; paranoid suspicion of near relatives.

Changes in mood: almost continual depression, interspersed with apathy, fatigue, severe tension, irrational fear.

Changes in behavior: occasional violence, suicide attempts, bizarre hatreds, outlandish emotional attachments.

Nobody knows for sure what causes these phenomena. One theory, focusing on the chemical origins of the disease, views the body as a malfunctioning "factory" that produces reality-distorting substances. This condition could well be inherited; any number of studies verify a genetic relationship among the diseased.

The schizophrenic may have suffered brain damage, before, after, or even during birth; there are indications that uterine trauma makes babies vulnerable. He could have suffered nutrient depletion at some point in life; poor eating habits, drug dependency, and impaired metabolism have all been shown to play some role.

For whatever reasons, the schizophrenic's metabolic machinery does not handle hormones, enzymes, and body nutrients normally.

The most comprehensive explanation of this chemical malfunctioning was first put forth in 1952 by Dr. Abram Hoffer and Dr. Humphrey Osmond, two psychiatrists who pioneered such investigations. Their extensive clinical research since then has validated their earliest experiments.

According to Hoffer and Osmond, schizophrenics convert epinephrine, a hormone produced by the adrenal gland, into at least two substances, adrenochrome and adrenolutin, both to an abnormal degree. These chemicals are hallucinogens. The schizophrenic needs no LSD to "see things": his body produces a similar drug.

Hoffer and Osmond subjected themselves to intravenous injections of adrenochrome to see what would happen. They reported that within ten minutes the ceiling of the laboratory seemed to change color, the light brightened intensely, and everything around them looked strangely changed.

Outside, the world seemed "sinister and unfriendly." Dr. Osmond said he felt "different" toward people and had to restrain himself from making nasty remarks. In a roadside diner he felt surrounded by "suspicious-looking" strangers who appeared to be spying on him.

Hallucinations? Of course. The very type experienced by schizophrenics.

Following the lead of Hoffer and Osmond, a small band of medical detectives has searched for further chemical clues. Several, including Dr. Robert Heath of Tulane University, have found a substance called *tarexin* in the blood of schizophrenics. Tarexin is thought to be a toxic protein ingredient that sensitizes a schizophrenic's brain to the two hallucinogenic chemicals Hoffer and Osmond had tested.

Herbert Y. Meltzer and John W. Crayton of the University of Chicago have found abnormal amounts of two enzymes (aldolase and creatine phosphokinase) in the blood streams of acute schizophrenics, and of all acute and some chronic psychotic patients. Suspecting an enzyme leakage from skeletal muscles, they performed muscle biopsies on psychotic patients and found supportive evidence. These muscle abnormalities are apt to affect the entire nervous system (brain and spinal cord) of both psychotic and schizophrenic patients.

The schizophrenic's faulty body chemistry is likely to show up on a glucose-tolerance test. From 50 to 75 percent are found to have hypoglycemia, and the fluctuating blood-sugar levels characteristic of this disorder magnify the distortions experienced by the schizophrenic. A single chocolate bar has been known to trigger a schizoid attack in some patients.

The special ways in which schizophrenics metabolize proteins, utilize various nutrients, secrete hormones, and manufacture enzymes are still being studied, and the evidence is incomplete. Yet clinicians using the biochemical approach have been overwhelmingly successful.

Hoffer and Osmond, having confirmed an overproduction of the two hallucinogenic compounds in schizophrenics, searched for a safe, effective counteragent. Vitamin B_3, as niacin (nicotinic acid) or niacinamide (nicotinamide), proved to be the sought-for nutrient. It was found to block the defect in body chemistry that overproduces the offending chemicals.

Testing massive doses of Vitamin B_3 on schizophrenics for more than twenty years has produced startling results. Niacin-based therapy has cured an astonishing 93 percent of Hoffer and Osmond's patients who had been ill less than two years; among patients with extended illnesses 87 percent have been cured; moreover, schizophrenics not receiving nicotinic acid have a suicide rate twenty-two times as high as that of the population at large, and schizophrenics treated with adequate supplies of nicotinic acid have a near-zero suicide rate.

Physicians practicing megavitamin therapy do not rely solely on vitamins. Depending on the patient, they may prescribe enzymes (administered orally or by injection), shock therapy, inhalation therapy, tranquilizers, antianxiety drugs, antidepressants, psychic energizers, lithium carbonate, or supportive psychotherapy. Corrective diets and complete multivitamin-mineral supplements are often prescribed in addition to the megadoses of niacin, vitamin C, and other vitamins.

Vitamin therapy holds a unique advantage over every other treatment plan: it meets the major medical qualification of doing no harm to the patient. There are no dangerous side effects. B_3 in the form of niacin (but not in the form of niacinamide) can cause some bothersome "flushing," a rash, headaches, or a transient fall in blood pressure; and both B_3 and C may occasionally cause some nausea or diarrhea. These reactions are temporary. (For full coverage of contraindications and side effects of niacin, see Appendix A.)

Since vitamins C and E are both antioxidants, their use in a megavitamin regime serves to suppress further the schizophrenic's production of hallucinogenic substances. Children often respond quickly—two to six months generally brings significant change.

The following daily dosages of vitamins are being used with other forms of therapy to treat schizophrenia:

Vitamin	Dosage
B_3 (niacin or niacinamide)	1-12 grams
C (ascorbic acid)	1-12 grams
B_6 (pyridoxine)	200-500 milligrams
B_1 (thiamine)	1-2 grams
E (d-alpha tocopherol)	400-1600 units
pantothenic acid	200-600 milligrams

A certain percentage of schizophrenic patients do not respond to any treatment, megavitamin therapy included. The four-day fast is Dr. Hoffer's latest approach, a tactic he has found successful with his hardest-to-treat patients. His work indicates that some schizophrenics may be highly allergic to substances found in many foods. Controlled fasting has been studied for more than twenty-five years at the Moscow Psychiatric Institute. Dr. Uri Nickolayev combats schizophrenia with long periods of complete food abstinence, followed by heavy vitamin doses and a gradual return to eating, starting with fruits and vegetables.

Few revolutions are bloodless. Radical new "methods against madness" have created conflicts between opposing theorists with no détente yet in sight. Wedded to earlier theories, the opposition has dug in its heels, scoffed at the success stories, jeered at published data. The resistance typifies the deep prejudice and inertia prevalent within the medical profession.

For schizophrenics and their families, to be caught up in the controversy can be a devastating experience. Dr. David Hawkins, whose success with nutritionally based therapy for alcoholism has been mentioned earlier, tells of such an instance.

A thirty-three-year-old housewife had been seriously schizophrenic for more than five years. Her wealthy family had funded a kind of psychiatric Cook's Tour in search of a cure; her condition grew progressively worse. When she reached a violent and suicidal stage, a frontal lobotomy was prescribed, indicating how hopeless her case had become. Before the irreversible operation was scheduled, her family asked that megavitamin therapy be tried.

The attending psychiatrist was outraged at the idea, but the family insisted. In ten weeks, after being given megavitamin therapy, thyroid extract, tranquilizers in small dosages, and a hypoglycemic diet, she was released. Fourteen months later she was completely recovered, taking care of household and children, socially active, holding a part-time job.

Can you be a latent schizophrenic and not know it?

Yes.

Is there hope for a permanent cure once the disease is discovered?

Again, the answer is yes.

Hoffer and Osmond designed a test to assess changes in perception, thought, and mood that generally signify the onset of schizophrenia. In the following simplified version, every healthy person will obtain some score, so don't be alarmed. A score over 30 is a warning to see a doctor; a score over 60 is a signal to seek immediate help.

Occasionally, teen-agers may score high even though mentally well. People with anxiety, personality disorders, psychoneuroses, manic depression, and other nonschizophrenic conditions may also score high.

This test does not conclusively prove the presence or absence of the disease. You must not presume to diagnose either yourself or anyone else as schizophrenic. The test can, however, alert you to the danger signs.

• Symptometer

Visual Perception	Score
People's faces sometimes pulsate as I watch them.	5
People's faces seem to change in size as I watch them.	5
When I look at things like tables and chairs they seem strange.	5
My hands or feet sometimes feel far away.	5
My hands or feet often look very small now.	5
Cars seem to move very quickly now. I can't be sure where they are.	5
When I am driving in a car, objects and people change shape very quickly. They didn't before.	5
People look as if they were dead now.	5
Lately I often get frightened when driving myself in a car.	5
People's eyes seem very piercing and frightening.	1
People watch me a lot more than they used to.	1
People watch me all the time.	1
I feel rays of energy upon me.	1
Most people have halos (areas of brightness) around their heads.	1
Sometimes I have visions of people when I close my eyes.	1
Sometimes I have visions of people during the day when my eyes are open.	1
Sometimes I have visions of animals or scenes.	1
Sometimes I have visions of God or of Christ.	1
Sometimes the world seems unreal.	1
Sometimes I feel very unreal.	1
When I look at people they seem strange.	1

Visual Perception	Score
Often when I look at people they seem to be like someone else.	1
Now and then when I look in the mirror my face changes and seems different.	1
My body now and then seems to be altered— too big or too small, out of proportion.	1
Sometimes the world becomes very bright as I look at it.	1
Sometimes the world becomes very dim as I look at it.	1
Sometimes when I read, the words begin to look funny. They move around or grow faint.	1
Sometimes when I watch TV the picture looks very strange.	1
Sometimes I feel there is a fog or mist shutting me away from the world.	1
Sometimes objects pulsate when I look at them.	1
Pictures appear to be alive and to breathe.	1
I often see sparks or spots of light floating before me.	1
My hands or feet sometimes seem much too large.	1
I sometimes feel that I have left my body.	1
I often feel I have left my body.	1
I get more frightened now when I am driven in a car by others.	1

Auditory Perception	
I often hear or have heard voices talking about or to me.	5
I have often heard strange sounds, e.g., laughing, which frighten me.	5
I have heard voices coming from radio, television, or tape recorders talking about me.	5
I often hear my thoughts inside my head.	5
I often hear my own thoughts outside my head.	5

Auditory Perception	**Score**
My sense of hearing is now more sensitive than it ever has been.	1
I now have more trouble hearing people.	1
I often have singing noises in my ears.	1
I have often felt that there was another voice in my head.	1
I hear my own thoughts as clearly as if they were a voice.	1

Tactile Perception	
I sometimes feel I am being pinched by unseen things.	5
My sense of touch has now become very keen.	1
I sometimes have sensations of crawly things under my skin.	1
I sometimes feel rays of electricity shooting through me.	1
Some of my organs feel dead.	1
I sometimes feel my stomach is dead.	1
I sometimes feel my bowels are dead.	1
I now have trouble feeling hot or cold things.	1
I sometimes feel strange vibrations shivering through me.	1
My bones often feel soft.	1

Taste Perception	
Some foods which never tasted funny before do so now.	1
I can taste bitter things in some foods, like poison.	1
Foods taste flat and lifeless.	1
I have more difficulty tasting foods now.	1
Water now has funny tastes.	1
Cigarettes taste queer now.	1

Olfactory Perception

Things smell very funny now.	5
Other people smell strange.	5
Other people's cigarette smoke smells strange—like a gas.	1
My body odor is much more noticeable than it once was.	1
My body odor is now much more unpleasant.	1
I sweat much more now than I used to.	1
I can no longer smell perfumes as well as I used to.	1
Foods smell funny now.	1

Time Perception

Time seems to have changed recently, but I am not sure how.	5
I can no longer tell how much time has gone by.	5
The days seem to go by very slowly.	1
Some days move by so quickly it seems only minutes have gone by.	1
I have much more trouble keeping appointments.	1
I have much more trouble getting my work done on time.	1
The world has become timeless for me.	1
I find that past, present, and future seem all muddled up.	1

Thought

There are some people trying to do me harm.	5
I can read other people's minds.	5
People interfere with my body to harm me.	5
People interfere with my mind to harm me.	5
I don't like meeting people. You can't trust anyone now.	5
Most people hate me.	5
I am not sure who I am.	5

Thought	Score
At times my mind goes blank.	1
At times my ideas disappear for a few minutes and then reappear.	1
I am bothered by very disturbing ideas.	1
My mind is racing away from me.	1
At times I am aware of people talking about me.	1
There is some plot against me.	1
I have a mission in life given to me by God.	1
At times some other people can read my mind.	1
At times when I come into a new situation, I feel strongly the situation is a repeat of one that happened before.	1
I now become easily confused.	1
I am now much more forgetful.	1
I now am sick.	1
I cannot make up my mind about things that before did not trouble me.	1
My thinking gets all mixed up when I have to act quickly.	1
I very often get directions wrong.	1
Strange people or places frighten me.	1
People are watching me.	1
I feel as if I were dead.	1
People are often envious of me.	1
Many people know that I have a mission in life.	1
People interfere with my body to help me.	1
People interfere with my mind to help me.	1
I know that most people expect a great deal of me.	1
More people admire me now than ever before.	1

Feelings and Emotions

I very often am very tired.	1
I very often suffer from severe nervous exhaustion.	1

Feelings and Emotions	Score
I very often have great difficulty falling asleep at night.	1
I usually feel alone and sad at a party.	1
I usually feel miserable and blue.	1
Life seems entirely hopeless.	1
I am very painfully shy.	1
I am often misunderstood by people.	1
I have to be on my guard with friends.	1
Very often friends irritate me.	1
My family irritates me very much.	1
I am often very shaky.	1
I am constantly keyed up and jittery.	1
Sudden noises make me jump or shake badly.	1
I often become scared of sudden movements or noises at night.	1

The higher the score, the more imperative it is to see a doctor who can determine the biochemical, physical, and psychological causes. The physical tests for schizophrenia include a general medical and neurological examination and a brain-wave test. Chemical tests should include the glucose-tolerance test for hypoglycemia, biochemical blood analyses, and blood or urine testing for toxic substances or other agents peculiar to schizophrenia.

The many possible physical causes that must be checked to diagnose schizophrenia correctly suggest that it is mislabeled a "mental" disease. It might more accurately be described as extreme metabolic dysperception.

No one practicing megavitamin therapy claims to have all the answers. No one can yet complete the sentence, "Vitamin B_3 therapy works because . . ." The proportion of schizophrenics cured by the treatments described in this chapter, however, is evidence enough that they should be tried.

As one totally recovered schizophrenic put it: "It's really not important to me how or why vitamin therapy works. What matters is that after eleven years of a living hell, I'm well."

6

Hypoglycemia, The Nondisease: Can a Sweet Tooth Lead to a Sour Disposition?

Memorandum to all legislators concerned with deteriorating mental health in the nation: It is recommended that accurate nutritional labeling be made mandatory.

Print on all candy wrappers the following warning: "This product can be dangerous to your mental health."

Label sugar-coated cereals with an X-rating: "More dangerous to children than pornography."

Tag sugar-laden processed foods with the skull and crossbones, a universally recognized symbol for "poison."

Post large red warning signs on vending machines that spew forth sugar-filled snacks: "Hazardous products within."

Keep refined sugar, like other dangerous weapons, under lock and key, to be sold only to licensed users.

Impose a high excise tax on "junk foods" to support inmates of mental institutions.

Are we serious? Very! The sugar-laden American diet has led to a national epidemic of hypoglycemia, an ailment characterized by irrational behavior, emotional instability, distorted judgment, and nasty personality defects. Almost 10 percent of the population is hypoglycemic.

The disease is full of paradoxes. One might reasonably assume that eating too much sugar would *raise* the level of sugar in the blood, but the body does not work in such a simple fashion. Instead, *low* blood sugar is the result.

Hypoglycemia is the exact opposite of diabetes; yet it is often the forerunner of that disease. In diabetes, too little usable insulin circulates in the blood stream; in hypoglycemia (also called hyperinsulinism), there is too much. An excess of this sugar-regulating hormone, released by the pancreas in response to a rapidly rising blood sugar, drives blood-sugar levels below normal, triggering a craving for sweets along with a variety of physical or mental symptoms.

An abnormal plunge in blood-sugar levels is perilous, sending shock waves through every cell in the body and affecting the nervous system and the brain most of all. An erratic mental state results, with a list of symptoms and complaints reading like a compendium on a bottle of snake-oil medicine: dizziness, fainting or blackouts, headaches, fatigue or exhaustion, drowsiness, narcolepsy (abnormal attacks of sleepiness), muscle pains and cramps, cold hands and feet, numbness, insomnia, nightmares, irritability, crying spells, restlessness, nervous breakdown, inability to concentrate, excessive worry and anxiety, depression, forgetfulness, illogical fears, suicidal thoughts, tremors, cold sweats, inner trembling, uncoordination, convulsion, fast and/or noticeable heart beat, blurred vision, allergies, itching and crawling sensations, neurodermatitis, arthritic pains, gastrointestinal upsets, loss of appetite, loss of sexual drive, and impotency.

Spells of low blood sugar give rise to other widely assorted difficulties: dry or burning mouth, ringing in the ears, poor memory, temper tantrums, noise and light sensitivity, shortness of breath, peculiar breath or perspiration odor, nausea, and hot flashes. A typical hypoglycemia victim is, in fact, an emotional yo-yo, strung out on a chemical reaction he cannot control, with reactions so severe they frequently resemble insanity.

This crazy-quilt pattern of symptoms is hard to diagnose, easy to pass off as "just an attack of nerves." Most hypoglycemics are regarded as "cranks" or "complainers" by their families, "hypochondriacs" by their doctors, "neurotics" by society. Milder cases are advised: "You'll get over it—eat something sweet when the craving hits." This is the worst thing a hypoglycemic can do, for the more sweets eaten, the more insulin is released, the lower the blood-sugar levels plunge, the more sugar is craved . . . on and on in a never-ending cycle.

Sweetened snack foods and drinks and white-flour products (refined carbohydrates) are the most deadly for hypoglycemics. A normal pancreas, through its insulin production, is able to keep the body's blood-sugar levels under control and in balance. But when it is habitually assaulted by these offending foods, it panics and produces too much insulin, causing blood-sugar levels to plunge downward.

Every tenth person inherits a supersensitive pancreas genetically incapable of handling large intakes of sugar. Such a pancreas overproduces insulin quite easily. Quickly overburdened, it loses all ability to function with precision and becomes an ineffective regulator.

The adrenal glands, which produce hormones that aid in returning low-blood-sugar levels to normal, react similarly. When relentless demands are made on them, they grow fatigued, and the hypoglycemic experiences a characteristic physical and mental exhaustion.

In 1949 the American Medical Association conferred its highest scientific award, the Distinguished Service Medal, on Dr. Seale Harris of Birmingham, Alabama, for research that led to the discovery of hypoglycemia. Dr. Harris was the first to observe that many patients who were not diabetic and had not been given insulin treatments appeared to go into "insulin shock." He also noted that some patients showed the same reactions as diabetics who accidentally overdosed themselves with insulin. Could these patients be overproducing insulin in their own bodies? His suspicion was confirmed, and, furthermore, he found that diet was frequently to blame.

Subsequent research has shown that common drugs can lead to

hypoglycemia. Medications such as anti-inflammatory drugs, analgesics, anticoagulants, antibiotics, diuretics, hormones, stimulants and tranquilizers, nicotine, alcohol, and a number of other
chemicals can alter blood-sugar levels. Caffeine can raise
blood-sugar levels in diabetics; but by stimulating insulin release, it
can lower blood-sugar levels in nondiabetics and hypoglycemics.

Habitual cocktail-partying can bring on hypoglycemia, especially if the partygoer skips a meal or two while on the circuit.
Alcohol also primes the pancreas so that refined carbohydrates
subsequently eaten produce hyperinsulinism. Other contributing
factors are chronic malnutrition, abnormal liver and kidney function, a deficiency of certain adrenal hormones, and a lack of trace
minerals such as chromium and manganese, which are essential for
carbohydrate and sugar metabolism.

Hypoglycemia has been found to be the result of *how* we eat as
well as *what* we eat. All too many Americans skip breakfast or start
the day with coffee and a sweet roll, followed by a cigarette. This
begins the hypoglycemic cycle once again. The combination of
caffeine, sugar, and nicotine triggers a flood of insulin into the
system. Blood-sugar levels first rise, then plummet some two or
three hours later, just in time for the midmorning coffee break.

More coffee, another pastry, a few more cigarettes, and our
victim feels better—temporarily. If by lunchtime his nerves demand
a quick drink or he skips that meal and satisfies his hunger with
more coffee, a sweet soft drink, or a heavily refined carbohydrate
repast, he will be tense, nervous, and irritable by two, in worse
shape by four, and even a well-balanced dinner will not restore his
physical and mental equilibrium. He is exhausted, yet he may get
only a few hours' sleep each night.

Campaigns designed to educate the public to the necessity of
starting the day with a good breakfast should not be regarded as
self-serving propaganda by whatever industry is sponsoring them.
Our metabolic machinery *demands* a good nutritional start to the
day. Some 15-20 grams of high-quality protein are necessary to
sustain blood-glucose levels during the morning.

The American Medical Association, after applauding Dr. Harris's findings more than two decades ago, did an astonishing turnabout in 1973. It labeled hypoglycemia a "nondisease," despite the experience of a large segment of the medical community that it is *the* common denominator in many emotional complaints.

It will take more than an AMA disclaimer to abolish hypoglycemia. It will take a radical change in the American diet.

Since 1890 our diet has undergone two technological disasters from which it has never recovered: the milling process, which strips off the outer bran coating and the wheat-germ kernel when grain is made into flour, thus eliminating vitamins, minerals, and essential amino acids; and the refinement of sugar into a "pure" white substance totally devoid of nutrients. Sugar cane in its natural form is an acceptable food, rich in nutrients. Refined white sugar is not only valueless, but a chemical menace, *for it lacks the very B vitamins and minerals necessary for its assimilation.* The body then steals the vitamins from other foods or from storage depots in the body, creating a B-complex and mineral deficiency—an important factor in emotional upset.

By 1940 many Americans were deriving almost two-thirds of their daily calories from devitalized refined carbohydrates (white rice, white flour, white sugar) and hydrogenated fats. Since then, matters have gotten much worse. At a recent National Foods Editors Conference in Chicago, Dr. Lawrence Power of Wayne State University disclosed the bad news: "As a nation, we now eat more than a hundred and twenty pounds of sugar per person per year."

"Not me," many readers will protest. Yet diet-conscious consumers do indeed contribute to this overall statistic, even as they carefully say "no thanks" to pies and cakes and take their coffee unsweetened.

How? They are eating "hidden sugar."

Do you put ketchup on your hamburger? There is sugar in it. Do you spread relish on your hot dog? There's sugar in that. Have a side dish of canned corn? Grab a quick lunch of canned soup? Snack on a frozen pizza? Sprinkle bottled salad dressing on your greens?

Check the labels on food items. If there is a listing of the contents, you will see that sugar is often one of the ingredients, even in the most unlikely products. Were you to shop diligently with an eye toward eliminating *every* food item containing sugar, you would have to scratch from your shopping list 90 percent of your normal purchases, including prepared baby food. A general rule of thumb is to avoid prepared "convenience" foods, since manufacturers put sugar in foods that the average housewife would never sweeten when preparing at home.

Dr. Michael Jacobson, director of the Center for Science in the Public Interest, estimates that about 19 percent of the average American's caloric intake comes from sugar. He recently released a chart showing the sugar content of sixty-five different fabricated foods. Some items contained as much as *68 percent sugar!* Even these disturbing figures are merely "guesstimates," for manufacturers very rarely disclose the precise sugar content of their products.

Another normally overlooked source of "hidden sugar" is liquid medicines, both prescription and nonprescription. According to a report prepared by two research pharmacists, John A. Bosso and Robert E. Pearson, from the School of Pharmacy and the Drug Information Services of the State University of New York at Buffalo, even a diabetic patient, whose sugar intake must be severely limited, may be ingesting from 10 to 15 percent of his prescribed allotment of carbohydrates through common medications.

They point out that "the Food and Drug Administration does not require complete disclosure of diluents, binders, fillers, flavoring agents, sweeteners, etc., in their labeling regulations." This situation is as much a problem for the hypoglycemic as for the diabetic.

Of great concern is the effect of hypoglycemia on children. Dr. Joseph Wilder of New York, a specialist in psychiatry and neurology, has found that:

In adults, faulty or insufficient nutrition may alter or impair specific or general mental functions and eventually cause structural damage of the central nervous system. In children, we face a grave additional factor. The development of the brain may be retarded, stopped, altered. . . . The child may be neurotic, psychopathic, and be subject to anxiety, running away tendencies, aggressiveness, a blind urge to activity and destructiveness, with impairment of moral sensibilities. In its simplest form, it is a tendency to deny everything, contradict everything, refuse everything, at any price.

Dr. Wilder's evaluation may help you to understand better the screaming, stamping children so often seen with a mother whose shopping cart is piled high with soda pop, cookies, candy, and baked goods.

Still another area of concern is the relationship that has been found between hypoglycemia and juvenile delinquency. In 1941, N. Rojas and A. F. Sanchi reported in the *Archives of Legal Medicine* that their examination of 129 delinquents convicted of offenses against persons and property revealed low blood sugar in all but thirteen.

Some adult crimes, including murder, may also be hypoglycemia-related. Dr. E. M. Abrahamson has found that the "brain waves of persons with low blood sugar are abnormal," and that "with chronic sugar starvation of the brain cells comes a fogged moral sense and distorted conceptions." Many suicides, too, may be caused by the profound depression and urge to escape from life that often characterize the hypoglycemic.

One forty-eight-year-old man, after brooding on his domestic difficulties for many weeks, concluded he could no longer go on living and compulsively drank a bottle of iodine. He was rushed to the hospital in time. Later, he was given a glucose-tolerance test, which revealed a serious hypoglycemic condition. With dietary correction, the man so improved that in less than three weeks after his aborted suicide he was back at work, feeling quite fit, and able to resolve his problems in a sensible and realistic fashion.

Dr. Sam E. Roberts, professor emeritus of the University of Kansas School of Medicine, believes that marital difficulties may frequently be aggravated by unsuspected hypoglycemia. In *Ex-*

haustion: Causes and Treatment, he recommends that any married couple thinking of divorce should take the low-blood-sugar test if one or the other is exhausted or their dispositions are combative or violent.

Hypoglycemia can endanger people who do not themselves suffer from the disease. Everyone who drives a car, rides the highways, or travels by commercial airline is vulnerable to the problems it precipitates. In heavy traffic someone with hypoglycemia may be suddenly overcome with disorders of vision, weakness, or blurred consciousness. By reacting incorrectly, he can easily cause an accident. Narcolepsy, an inability to resist sleep, may also be the result of a falling blood glucose level. "Asleep at the wheel" is not usually specified on death certificates.

As for airline pilots, Dr. Charles R. Harper, former regional medical director for United Airlines, tested 175 pilots over the age of forty and found evidence of low-blood-sugar conditions in 44 of them. Dr. Harper suggests that airline stewardesses could contribute further to aviation safety if they stopped shuttling back and forth to the cockpit with coffee, soft drinks, and sweet rolls for the vulnerable pilots.

Many people first suspect the real cause of their nervous, overwrought condition after reading about hypoglycemia. If you are suspicious that you might be an undetected hypoglycemic, it is time to face up to the possibility and seek accurate verification.

A simple, self-administered questionnaire that can help you to make a pre-diagnosis has been devised by Dr. John F. Bumpus, a Denver physician-surgeon. You might like to take it for yourself, a family member, or a friend.

The instructions are very simple: to indicate degree of severity, use figure 1 for mild, 2 for moderate, and 3 for severe. Check only those symptoms that apply to your case. Leave blanks where answers do not apply.

Health Appraisal Indicator

1. _____ abnormal craving for sweets
2. _____ afternoon headaches
3. _____ alcohol consumption
4. _____ allergies—tendency to asthma, hay fever, skin rash, etc.
5. _____ awaken after few hours' sleep—hard to get to sleep
6. _____ aware of breathing heavily
7. _____ bad dreams
8. _____ bleeding gums
9. _____ blurred vision
10. _____ brown spots or bronzing of skin
11. _____ bruise easily ("black and blue" spots)
12. _____ "butterfly" stomach, cramps
13. _____ can't decide easily
14. _____ can't start in A.M. before coffee
15. _____ can't work under pressure
16. _____ chronic fatigue
17. _____ chronic nervous exhaustion
18. _____ convulsions
19. _____ crave candy or coffee in afternoons
20. _____ cry easily for no reason
21. _____ depressed
22. _____ dizziness
23. _____ drink _____ cups of coffee daily
24. _____ eat often or get hunger pains or faintness
25. _____ eat when nervous
26. _____ faintness if meals delayed
27. _____ fatigue, eating relieves
28. _____ fearful
29. _____ get "shaky" if hungry
30. _____ hallucinations
31. _____ hand tremor
32. _____ heart palpitates if meals missed or delayed

33. _____ highly emotional
34. _____ hunger between meals
35. _____ insomnia
36. _____ inward trembling
37. _____ irritable before meals
38. _____ lack energy
39. _____ magnify insignificant events
40. _____ moods of depression, "blues" or melancholy
41. _____ poor memory
42. _____ reduced initiative
43. _____ sleepy after meals
44. _____ sleepy during day
45. _____ weakness, dizziness
46. _____ worrier, feel insecure
47. _____ symptoms come before breakfast? (answer yes or no)
48. _____ do you feel better after breakfast than before? (answer yes or no)

Finished? Now add up the points you have inserted in the blanks. Having observed thousands of these scores, Dr. Bumpus has concluded that anyone with a total score of 25 or more should be tested further for hypoglycemia. Some symptoms are more diagnostic than others. If you answered any three of the following questions, 16, 17, 24, 26, 27, 29, 43, or 44, you are likely to be suffering at least *some* sugar intolerance.

If the Health Appraisal Indicator suggests the likelihood of functional hypoglycemia (or reactive hypoglycemia, as some prefer to call it), a five- or six-hour glucose-tolerance test is indicated. It is generally begun at 8:00 A.M., following a twelve-hour fast (from 8:00 P.M. the evening before). After the initial blood sample is drawn, the patient swallows 100 grams of glucose. Blood samples are taken thirty and sixty minutes later, and at hourly intervals for five or six hours. Special diets prior to testing are not necessary but, if possible, all medications (such as tranquilizers) that affect the blood-sugar level should be discontinued several days before the test. No tobacco, food, drink, or physical activity is allowed during the test.

Anyone can be "on the way" to hypoglycemia if he continues to stuff himself with unwholesome foods, and a corrective diet is a must for the diagnosed hypoglycemic. This "hypoglycemic" diet can best be described as relatively *high* in complete (animal) protein, moderate in fat content (roughly balanced between saturated and unsaturated fats), moderate in total carbohydrate content, and low in the rapidly assimilated carbohydrates.

It is important to avoid certain foods completely: sugar, honey, dried fruit, products such as noodles, macaroni, spaghetti, pizza, white bread, biscuits, rolls, crackers (all items made from refined white flour), all sweets and desserts (except fresh fruit), all sugar-sweetened soft drinks, foods and drinks containing caffeine, and alcoholic beverages. Potatoes, corn, rice, peas, lima beans, and baked beans may also have to be restricted or avoided.

Many versions of the original "Seale Harris Diet" for hypoglycemia have been published under other names. A modification by Cincinnati psychiatrist Dr. H. M. Salzer is one good example (see Appendix C for the complete diet).

Medicines taken by a hypoglycemic should be caffeine-free. A quick glance at the label or a call to your pharmacist will reveal whether any medication contains off-limits ingredients.

Changing your eating habits radically may seem to require an alteration in life style too drastic to contemplate. At first, your reaction may be, "All the fun in eating is gone. I'd rather be sick."

Give the diet a chance. Your body is smarter than you suspect, and you will not have to exercise a will of iron for the rest of your life. After a relatively short period of strict adherence to the new regime, you'll find you have lost your taste and craving for the forbidden foods. Many patients have confessed to fudging on their diets during a holiday spree, only to find that these foods tasted "sickly sweet," not at all as good as they remembered them.

For hypoglycemics, a nourishing breakfast is particularly essential to prevent fatigue and promote efficiency during the day.

Dr. W. D. Currier of Pasadena, California, has his patients start the day with a fortified breakfast eggnog:

1 or 2 glasses of nonfat milk
1 or 2 raw eggs
1 or 2 tablespoons of powdered skim milk
1 tablespoon of brewer's yeast powder
1 tablespoon of wheat germ and/or rice polishings
1 tablespoon of lecithin granules
1 tablespoon of desiccated liver
1 tablespoon cold-processed safflower or corn oil

Blend by hand or in an electric mixer. Add flavorings as desired. Ingredients should be kept refrigerated. Supplies 350–400 calories and about 60 grams of protein.

This is an excellent recipe, *except* for those hypoglycemics who have difficulty digesting milk. A good vitamin-mineral supplement aids recovery (see the formula listed in Chapter 13). Megadoses of certain nutrients, particularly B_3, or niacin, can help stabilize blood-glucose levels. Pyridoxine (vitamin B_6) can help the niacin to work more effectively, and those hypoglycemics who are continually troubled by excess fatigue may benefit from a wheat-germ-oil supplement at mealtime.

Since hypoglycemia is clearly not the only condition that can cause the symptoms we have described, it is always wise to consult a nutritionally knowledgeable doctor. Many frustrated hypoglycemics have had to doctor themselves, and some who have recovered feel that they should help others.

One patient, Mrs. B., came under our care at about the same time that she found her way to a lay-oriented organization known as "Neurotics Anonymous," which operates very much like Alcoholics Anonymous. A number of factors complicated her life, not the least of which were her hectic working schedule and many career tensions. At home she attempted to cope with multiple responsibilities to husband and children.

"I got to the point where I felt there was not enough of me to go around," she said.

Mrs. B.'s list of physical complaints matched her emotional stresses: digestive upsets, insomnia, periods of near exhaustion. She had visited many doctors over a period of ten years, all of whom had found nothing physically wrong with her.

"I got tired of hearing that I was a 'compulsive' worker, beset with 'guilts,' raised to be an 'overachiever,' and now suffering from a female psychological ailment known as 'fear of success,'" she complained.

Discovering that she had hypoglycemia, we placed her on a corrective nutritional regime. The improvement was so dramatic that her fellow "neurotics" noticed the change and demanded that she share the secrets of her "miracle" cure.

"I used to just sympathize with friends and neighbors who were breaking down under psychological stress," she said at the time of her last visit to us. "Now, when a girl friend complains about her husband's being lazy, drinking too much, or being short-tempered, I ask about his eating habits instead. When a friend tells me her child is a behavior problem, I'm likely to criticize her food-shopping habits, not the quality of her 'mothering.' And when someone at the office flares up and is abusive, my question is, 'What in the world are you eating that's making you act that way?'

"This has become my own private 'food for thought' program. I feel it's the least I can do to help others who are suffering as needlessly as I once was."

The statistics show that:

One in ten suffers low-blood-sugar problems.

One in ten is a candidate for mental illness.

Coincidence? We think not. There is overwhelming evidence that life for everyone would be considerably improved if this one nutritional disorder, hypoglycemia, were attacked and conquered.

7

"Mental" Illness:
The Twilight Zone

Nobody would ever call Bobby Perkins (not his real name) a "mental" case. Most people would probably consider him an average guy.

A successful thirty-seven-year-old building contractor, he credits his achievements to "drive" and an understanding of human nature: "I'm not afraid of hard work, and I never let anyone get too close to me. You just can't trust people—except, maybe your wife."

He realizes he has some destructive habits: "Sometimes I'll booze it up all day, with no one the wiser. Once in a while I go on a bender. Sometimes I don't feel like drinking at all. I guess I smoke too much, but hell, it takes the edge off things."

He's forgotten what it's like to feel top-notch: "I'm not too bad off. A lot of people are probably in worse shape. Maybe I go at things too hard. I guess I don't know how to take it easy. A man with a family to support has to really keep pushing—or else. I never told anyone before, but sometimes I feel like I'm going to crack up."

Mr. Perkins's case history divulged a number of other difficulties: frequent, severe headaches, chronic nervousness, more often depressed than not. He blamed the stress of circumstances for most of his miseries and accepted them as inevitable: "I'll bet most of the guys in my business feel as rotten as me. They just don't talk about it."

Mr. Perkins is right in assuming that many of his fellow contractors are also silent sufferers, but he is wrong in thinking his business is to blame. Blue-collar workers, white-collar workers, professionals, and the unemployed all may live in the "twilight zone" of not-so-obvious mental illness. Many can fill a calendar with a complaint a day: Monday, a bad headache; Tuesday, mad-at-the-world; Wednesday, dizziness; Thursday, a sleepless night; Friday, the "shakes"; Saturday, out of sorts; Sunday, too tired to enjoy a day off.

Physicians usually classify such minor physical and mental complaints as a run-down condition brought about by stress or overwork; psychiatrists are apt to call them "psychosomatic."

A prescribed vacation will help even less than a session "on the couch." Neither approach comes to grips with the most prevalent cause of this patchwork pattern of problems: "mini" nutritional deficiency.

Vitamin C shortages are not considered critical until scurvy develops; B-vitamin depletions are not recognized as serious until there is a clear case of beriberi or pellagra; Vitamin B_{12} is neglected until pernicious anemia develops; vitamin E insufficiencies get particularly short shrift, since E is a vitamin in search of a disease.

Relatively few people suffer from the most easily diagnosed nutritional ailments. The majority limp through the haze that lies between the daylight of optimal health and the darkness of absolute illness, trying to cope with varying degrees of mental disability.

People don't "go crazy" suddenly, although they may appear to. Only bones crack from one sharp blow. Prior to an emotional breakdown, chemical imbalances have progressively worsened. The patient has grown increasingly anxious, developed additional physical and emotional symptoms so diversified that they defy a physical diagnosis but fit nicely into psychiatry's dictionary.

About 5 percent of the population suffers from what psychiatrists call *anxiety neurosis*. Typical symptoms include nervousness, exaggerated fears, sleep disturbances, general pervasive feelings of impending doom, loss of appetite.

One young patient described the way she felt: "I get all uptight for no good reason. I feel like I have a heavy lump of dough in my stomach. I get clammy and find it hard to breathe, like I'm going to have a heart attack. I've been told it's just nerves."

In standard psychiatric textbooks, physiological responses to chronic anxiety conditions are attributed to childhood trauma. A person "suffering from an anxiety reaction," according to one authoritative text, "invariably reveals that his parents were unable to give him constant, mature affection and protection from stress so that he suffered repeated exposure to unpleasant tensions. As a result, he lived in an unstable and uncomfortable emotional atmosphere from which he could never learn to face some of the dangers and responsibilities of ordinary living."

All of which may well be true. And yet, consider for a moment the *biochemical* underpinnings of anxiety neurosis. Patients with this condition may have exceptionally high levels of lactic acid (or lactate) in the blood, especially after strenuous physical activity.

How do people develop excess blood lactate? An underlying calcium deficiency is quite likely to be at fault, for high levels of lactic acid and insufficient calcium are correlated chemical abnormalities. Lactic acid binds the calcium, effectively imprisoning it. When too little calcium is circulating in the blood stream to spark the nervous system, palpitation, sweating, a racing heart, and "nerves" are the natural result. Enter your "anxiety neurotic."

In experiments at the Washington University School of Medicine, researchers first triggered acute anxiety reactions in subjects by injecting them with a lactate solution, and then effectively reduced the anxiety symptoms by injecting calcium.

Dr. John Wozny, a University of Alberta psychiatrist, has found that calcium therapy works wonders for the anxiety-ridden. One of his patients, a thirteen-year-old with a long history of emotional complaints, was a bundle of nerves. Tense and friendless, tortured by morbid fears, she particularly dreaded test days at school. Other psychiatrists who treated her had attributed her symptoms to an insecure family atmosphere.

Dr. Wozny tested for a nutritional disorder and recommended a high-calcium diet. Twenty-three days later the girl's fears and anxieties were overcome, she was able to get a full night's sleep, and she showed marked improvement at school.

When fourteen-year-old Larry came to Dr. Wozny, he was a nail-biting, fidgety adolescent, afraid to sleep without a light on, plagued by assorted aches and pains. The prescribed high-calcium diet had the boy feeling much better in three weeks. Larry, skeptical by nature, found it hard to believe a mere change in diet could be responsible for so dramatic an improvement. He cheated to see if his "shrink" had fooled him with "chemical mumbo jumbo"; in three days all his old symptoms, including stiff neck muscles, were back. Now fully convinced, he promised to stick to his calcium-rich diet.

A tiny decrease of calcium in the blood can produce uncontrollable temper outbursts. The very young are extremely vulnerable. Babies have been known to hold their breath and turn blue; toddlers often have outrageous tempers. If a youngster tends to have tantrums, the distracted mother might well consider the possibility of calcium deficiency before deciding her "behavior problem" needs a good spanking.

Calcium deficiencies generally sneak up slowly. Normally the body protects itself from blood-level fluctuations by drawing upon bone and muscle reserves. If this were not so, one day on a low-calcium diet would result in erratic nervous reactions. But the nervous system cannot continue "stealing" calcium indefinitely; eventually the balance must be restored with calcium-rich foods.

Sudden, unexpected emotional stress or heavy physical exertion can raise lactate levels, thereby depleting circulating calcium, in healthy people. You can protect yourself from the resulting nervous attacks by keeping your calcium reserves high. Extra calcium from cheese and other dairy products is easily come by, and calcium supplements are readily available.

In anxiety neurosis, as in so many other emotional ailments, vitamin deficiencies play an important part. "If all the vitamin B_3 were removed from our foods, everyone would become psychotic within one year," Dr. Hoffer has noted. A *total* lack of vitamin B_3 leads to pellagra, but *low* levels produce humorless, overemotional, down-in-the-dumps individuals who are rarely recognized for what they are: "minipellagrins."

To date, no method has been devised to determine precise niacin levels in the blood or brain cells. The late Dr. Tom Spies, an internationally famous nutritionist, developed his method of detecting vitamin B_3 deficiencies. Whenever he saw patients who were short-tempered and "swimmy-headed," he told them a funny story. If he couldn't get a laugh, he suspected a niacin deficiency. After hundreds of trials he learned that one of the early signs of niacin depletion is the loss of a sense of humor.

Today's teen-agers are noticeably less lighthearted than those of a generation ago. And the teen-age diet, coincidentally or not, suffers serious lacks of this vital nutrient. If nothing quite seems funny to you these days, don't be too quick to blame the morning news. Plentiful servings of raw green vegetables, whole grain cereals, eggs, organ meats, and nuts might help get you laughing again.

"How much B_3 is enough?" people frequently ask us.

There's no simple answer. Needs vary from person to person and even from day to day. The only sure-fire way to overcome or avoid depletion is to consume daily doses of nutrients several-fold the levels specified as "recommended daily allowances."

We have found the Recommended Dietary Allowances chart published by the National Research Council to be unreliable. For one thing, RDA standards have fluctuated capriciously from year to year both in the nutrients listed and the levels advised. Between 1964 and 1974, one of the B-complex vitamins (pantothenic acid) was first not listed, then listed at 5 milligrams, then taken off the next list, then put back on at 10 milligrams, and, in the latest edition, taken off completely.

Rarely does anyone fit the "average requirement" mold, anyway. When we checked the RDA of 500 milligrams per day for tryptophane (the amino-acid precursor of niacin) on a group of so-called normal adults, we found it too low for emotional well-being. *Twice* that amount was not enough for many subjects. Even those consuming 1000 milligrams per day experienced more numerous emotional difficulties than those regularly consuming higher amounts.

The records of daily food intake and the mental-health questionnaires filled out by each member of our study group clearly showed an inverse relationship between tryptophane consumption and emotional complaints: increased tryptophane intake, decreased complaints. Sixty-six of our research participants voluntarily increased their daily tryptophane intake, and the entire group was retested some months later. Those who had gone from an average 1001 milligrams per day to an average of 1331 milligrams showed a remarkable decrease in the number of psychological complaints. Subjects who had not increased their dosage remained virtually unchanged.

Two conclusions follow: the RDA for tryptophane has been set too low, and the millions of people whose diets provide only RDA levels or less are being mentally penalized.

The same is true for other nutritional elements. Skimpy supplies threaten sanity. Each substance plays a small but distinctive role in psychic functioning.

Take zinc, for example. Recent research has uncovered the fact that school children with poor appetites, slow growth rates, and a subnormal sense of taste and smell are suffering from zinc deficiencies.

This has also been found to be the case with students who were lethargic and apathetic about their school work. It is interesting to note that in an experiment conducted at the University of Michigan, in which students' hair was analyzed for trace minerals, those with the highest academic grades were found to have substantial amounts of zinc and copper in their systems.

According to Dr. Robert I. Henken of the National Heart and Lung Institute, zinc supplements have effectively restored taste and smell losses in 103 patients. The half a million persons in the United States who suffer from this perceptual difficulty are normally classified as psychiatric cases.

Zinc deficiency is more prevalent than supposed. Food refinement and zinc-depleted soils produce zinc-depleted plants, fruits, vegetables, grains, and animals. Dietary zinc supplements and complete mineral or vitamin supplements containing zinc are one answer. Foods from the sea, particularly herring, oysters, and sardines, offer plentiful supplies. Nuts and seeds are also good sources of zinc.

The brain needs only tiny amounts of zinc and other trace minerals to carry out its functions, and until quite recently serious deficiencies occurred only under bizarre circumstances. Changing food supplies and food technology have made the unusual commonplace, and the consequences can be serious. A French scientist who has studied areas designated by geological survey maps as having zinc-depleted soils found statistically significant higher suicide rates in those regions.

Today's motto: "Think zinc."

As with zinc, so with magnesium. Deficiencies are no longer rare. Magnesium is vital for nerve conduction, muscular contraction, and the transmission of impulses all along the nervous system.

Dr. Willard A. Krehl of the University of Iowa, analyzing a group of patients with *mild* magnesium deficiencies, found that 22 percent had convulsions; 44 percent suffered hallucinations; 78 percent evidenced mental confusion; 83 percent were disoriented, couldn't remember where they were, the year, the day, the month; and 100 percent startled easily and were alarmed by unexpected movement or noise.

Dr. Krehl's subsequent appeals for increased attention to the magnesium levels of disturbed patients, and for better laboratory procedures to detect inadequacies, fell on deaf ears until doctors at a well-equipped hospital created a psychiatric disaster by unwittingly inducing a severe magnesium deficiency in a patient. They made medical news with their report, which noted that their search of the literature uncovered *no previous mention* that hypomagnesia, by itself, causes brain dysfunctioning.

Their patient had been hospitalized for a bleeding ulcer, and the treatment, intravenous injection and gastric suction, controlled the bleeding. The patient, however, began behaving peculiarly. First irritable and uncooperative, he gradually became abusive and disoriented. By the sixth evening he was angrily accusing the hospital staff of enjoying his suffering, was given to angry outbursts and jumping at the slightest sound.

Laboratory tests continued to show his metabolic status to be "normal," but his mental state grew worse. Soon he was suffering tics, tremors, slurred speech, and an inability to stand up. New testing finally uncovered the magnesium deficiency, and immediate injections of magnesium sulfate brought a rapid recovery.

The physicians noted that the psychiatric changes that were among the first to appear were the last to *disappear*. This observation validated Dr. Krehl's belief that magnesium deficiency must be investigated when "mental" symptoms surface.

A heartening number of biochemically oriented psychiatrists have taken notice of recent developments and urged their Freudian colleagues to refocus on the physical conditions that lead to psychological dysfunction. At the 1972 meeting of the American Psychiatric Association, their fellow members were warned to take more seriously the responsibilities they undertake when they carry an "M.D." after their names.

All too frequently, a patient's psyche is probed while his physical condition is ignored. Take the case of a woman who had undergone psychotherapy for nine years. Her psychiatric history was a classic text of analytic theory, her medical history a blank page, when she came under the care of a more astute psychiatrist. An immediate neurological examination revealed a brain tumor so advanced that the woman died before an operation could be scheduled. "Unfortunately," this psychiatrist summed up, "many of us fail to use our medical training."

Even when rather common physical disorders which are known to precipitate "psychiatric" behavior could be the cause (such as hypothyroidism), psychiatrists habitually fail to order the necessary medical examinations. Those who fail to discover brain tumors and endocrine disturbances are not likely to uncover elusive conditions like the nutrient deficiencies we have been discussing.

How often does this happen?

A highly placed American Psychiatric Association official who made an in-depth study of the subject told us privately: "It borders on malpractice. Not five percent of practicing psychiatrists—that's a generous estimate—ever ask a patient anything about his medical history. It may take twenty-five years, but eventually they'll have buried themselves in their psychoanalytic theories. Psychiatry will be taken over by scientists who understand biochemistry and metabolic medicine."

In an informal survey of psychiatrists in the Washington, D.C., area he found that *not one* had ever requested medical information of any sort when accepting a new patient for treatment. Only rarely did they ask a patient if he was taking any drugs before prescribing their own favorite medication, despite the possibility that their prescription could be fatally incompatible with something already in the patient's medicine chest.

Psychiatry is far from the precise science many believe it to be. Dr. Larry Sharpe and his research colleagues at the Biometrics Research Institute have published numerous well-documented (and well-buried) reports showing that in study after study, psychiatrists throughout the country have been found to be at odds with one another when diagnosing the *same* patient.

Dr. George Watson, in *Nutrition and Your Mind*, takes a dim view of standard psychiatric diagnostic techniques. He points out that classifying patients according to vague and ill-defined symptoms tends to lump together people with vastly different underlying ailments. Even the most severely disturbed psychiatric cases are likely to be quite different metabolically. He has called for the development of metabolic profiles as a forerunner of more accurate diagnosis and treatment.

There are obviously many factors which cause emotional complaints: you could be suffering hidden nutrient deficiencies or any number of abnormalities involving hormones, electrolytes, blood gases, toxins, and a host of substances that doctors are only beginning to understand.

Can you be suffering a subclinical nutrient deficiency and not realize it? Of course.

Dr. David P. Goldberg has devised a test to spot early signs of mental and emotional distress. A unique feature of this "General Health Questionnaire," published in *The Detection of Psychiatric Illness by Questionnaire*, is that it can detect hidden psychiatric illnesses.

Are you ready to take a critical look at yourself? Then answer these thirty-six questions taken from the GHQ by circling either yes or no. These questions are concerned with your condition during the past few weeks, not months or years ago.

Have you been feeling that you are not well or in good
health? yes no

Have you been feeling in need of a good tonic? yes no

Have you been feeling run-down and out of sorts or
irritable? yes no

Have you felt that you are ill? yes no

Have you had trouble concentrating on whatever you are
doing? yes no

Have you been waking early and unable to go back to
sleep? yes no

Have you been getting up feeling your sleep hasn't re-
freshed you? yes no

Have you lost much sleep over worry? yes no

Have you been feeling mentally dull and sluggish? yes no

Have you been feeling that you have less energy and tire
easily? yes no

Have you had difficulty in going to sleep? yes no

Have you been restless and disturbed at night? yes no

Have you been unable to keep yourself busy doing
things? yes no

Have you been losing interest in your ordinary activities?	yes	no
Have you felt much of the time that you were not doing things well?	yes	no
Have you been dissatisfied with the way you get things done?	yes	no
Have you felt rather useless?	yes	no
Have you had trouble making decisions?	yes	no
Have you felt you are not able to make a start on anything?	yes	no
Have you felt yourself dreading everything that you have to do?	yes	no
Have you felt constantly under pressure or strain?	yes	no
Have you felt that you couldn't overcome your difficulties?	yes	no
Have you been finding life a struggle all the time?	yes	no
Have you been unable to enjoy your normal day-to-day activities?	yes	no
Have you been taking things pretty hard?	yes	no
Have you been getting scared or panicky for no good reason?	yes	no
Have you found it difficult to face up to your problems?	yes	no
Have you found everything getting too much for you?	yes	no
Have you been feeling unhappy and depressed?	yes	no
Have you been losing confidence in yourself?	yes	no
Have you been thinking of yourself as a worthless person?	yes	no
Have you felt that life is entirely hopeless?	yes	no
All things considered, have you found that you are not happy?	yes	no
Have you been feeling nervous and hung-up all the time?	yes	no
Have you felt that life isn't worth living?	yes	no

Have you found at times you couldn't do anything because
    your nerves were too bad?   yes   no

Add up your yes answers. The test indicates a general condition, not an exact diagnosis, but a score of seven or more indicates you should seek professional counsel.

Remember Bobby Perkins? He's learned a great deal since the day he first walked into our office, certain that his emotional difficulties were caused by his business success. Examinations revealed that he as yet had no serious condition, but that there were many minimal deficiencies working together to destroy his emotional well-being. We placed him on the Optimal Diet and prescribed a complete vitamin-mineral supplement along with some extra niacin, ascorbic acid, and vitamin B_6. He's lost his "shakes," his belligerence, his headaches, his nervousness, his stomach troubles, his frequent colds, and his dandruff. He's out of the "twilight zone."

Although we have only skimmed the surface of the hundreds of easily overlooked physical and nutritional ailments that mimic psychiatric problems, those we have discussed are evidence enough to make you wary of standard diagnoses of "mental" complaints. A metabolically oriented psychiatrist is likely to order a glucose tolerance test, a urine analysis, chest x-ray, a serological test for syphilis, and blood tests for cholesterol, protein bound iodine, potassium, sodium, calcium, magnesium, phosphorous, zinc, triglyceride and uric acid, and carbon dioxide before asking you about your mother.

The wisest course to follow when faced with even minor emotional difficulties is to seek help from a professional who will treat not just your mind but seek to correct any underlying difficulties (defects in body chemistry).

8

Drug-Induced Mental Illness: Psychodietetic Help for the Addicted

Mary, Carla, and Dorothy are rehashing the morning news headlines. The kids are off to school, the beds are made: it's coffee klatsch time in the suburbs.

"They raided the college dorms not twelve miles from here last night and picked up fifty pounds of marijuana. Twenty-three students were arrested as pushers. I dread the day my kids are old enough to leave home."

"What makes you think they're safe at junior high? I hear they've got a drug problem there too, but the school officials just won't admit it."

"Do you suppose *our* kids could be taking stuff? I kind of snoop around Stevie's room from time to time. I don't know what I'd do if I found he was hiding something."

Someone ought to do something, the trio agreed.

The drug problem *is* getting awfully close to home, closer than any of these women would be willing to admit.

Mary fumbles for a cigarette upon awakening each morning.

Carla "can't get started" without coffee.

Dorothy "needs" her predinner cocktail and the "occasional" tranquilizer to get through the day.

All three women are *everyday addicts*, and none of them knows it.

In the years since LSD and marijuana became household words, American parents have learned to dread a bewildering variety of chemical compounds. People who couldn't spell "psychedelic" a decade ago now shudder over a familiar list of hallucinogens with a fear they once reserved for kidnappers and child molesters.

Hidden in their cloud of apprehension is the astonishing truth that caffeine, nicotine, alcohol, and other legal drugs cause more damage to mind and body than all psychoactive drugs combined.

Mary knows she smokes too much. Carla admits she ought to cut down on the coffee. Dorothy is aware that her drinking and pill-popping might get out of hand. Yet none of them sees herself as an addict; none of them realizes that an addict is any person who habitually uses chemical agents to avoid the real or imagined physical and psychological consequences of abstinence.

Viewed in this light, even a few extra cups of coffee each day indicate the true nature of a "rational" habit: it is a drug addiction.

The drug, caffeine, is also found in tea, cola drinks, cocoa, and chocolate. It is one of the xanthines, a class of chemicals that, by stimulating the central nervous system, causes brain and spinal-cord disturbances. Two or three cups of coffee contain enough caffeine to stimulate the cerebral cortex of the brain, sharpen the senses, distort muscular coordination, and hamper timing.

Heavy coffee drinkers experience the three distinct signs of addiction: tolerance for the drug, withdrawal symptoms when it is removed, and craving after deprivation. Caffeine's addictive properties have been confirmed by many studies.

At the Stanford University School of Medicine, Dr. Avram Goldstein and Dr. Sophia Kaizer studied 239 young married women and their coffee-drinking habits. The heaviest users, those who routinely drank five or more cups of coffee each day, told the investigators why they invariably began their day with coffee: "I need it to get started in the morning," "I need it to give me a lift," "to calm my nerves," "for stimulation," "to give me energy," "because it's a habit." Each answer reveals the "need" that spells addiction.

These heavy coffee drinkers exhibited typical withdrawal symptoms when they gave up coffee: headaches, irritability, nerv-

Drug Induced Mental Illness • 103

ousness, restlessness, and inability to work effectively, compounded by lethargy. Drinking a cup of coffee promptly relieved their withdrawal symptoms.

Caffeinism, which leads to what is commonly called "coffee nerves," has often been misdiagnosed as a psychological ailment.

Dr. John F. Greden, an army psychiatrist, found this to be the case with a twenty-seven-year-old army nurse, married to an army physician, who complained of severe headaches, an irregular heartbeat which disturbed her several times each day, tremulous feelings, and lightheadedness.

Army psychiatrists had prescribed daily tranquilizers. She was suffering, they explained, from an anxiety reaction to her husband's imminent transfer to Vietnam.

Unwilling to accept this evaluation, she told Dr. Greden she was positive there was some other cause. "I'm not up-tight over John," she assured him, "and I'm not worried about our future either. I have the distinct feeling that it's something I'm eating, but I don't know what."

After examining her diet over the past three weeks, the period during which her symptoms had gradually developed, she and Dr. Greden traced their onset to the purchase of a new coffee pot. The coffee tasted so much better that she had begun drinking ten to twelve cups of strong black coffee every day. As soon as she stopped drinking the coffee, all her nervous symptoms disappeared.

Dr. Greden then discovered other patients whose caffeinism had been overlooked. Their symptoms also vanished after caffeine consumption was either eliminated or drastically reduced.

Anxiety symptoms can be brought about by coffee-drinking not generally considered excessive. One to three cups can produce an emotional reaction: even *one* cup of coffee contains 90 milligrams of caffeine. At least 25 percent of Americans over the age of seventeen drink *six* or more cups of coffee or tea each day. Enough coffee was sold in 1970 to provide the nation with 180 billion doses of caffeine!

We conducted a study of coffee and tea drinkers and found that a significantly higher number of psychological complaints existed among persons drinking seven or more cups of coffee each day than among those whose intake was more moderate.

Caffeine intake is boosted by the consumption of cola drinks, cocoa preparations, chocolate-flavored foods, and many pain remedies. A chocolate bar weighing one ounce contains approximately 20 milligrams of caffeine; some over-the-counter aspirin compounds contain 15 to 30 milligrams; and prescribed preparations to relieve your pain or keep you awake average 100 milligrams or more.

Caffeine, by stimulating insulin secretion, causes blood-sugar levels to drop. A hypoglycemic condition may be the result. Many of the psychological complaints common to hypoglycemics are similar to the ones Dr. Greden relieved by taking his patients off coffee.

If you suspect that coffee nerves may be contributing to your emotional difficulties, the Optimal Diet will help. It is designed to set your metabolic house in order, reduce the craving for caffeine and other drugs, and alleviate the withdrawal symptoms so often experienced by those who try to curtail their coffee consumption. Once you have improved your diet along the lines advised, you'll find it much easier to overcome the "I can't live without my coffee" syndrome.

Few people consider smoking a cause of emotional problems, yet nicotine, which is absorbed into the blood stream, adds to metabolic dysfunctioning. Nicotine disturbs the digestive system by impairing vitamin C absorption, and interferes with blood circulation. By constricting the blood vessels, nicotine robs the brain of its supply of essential nutrients, particularly its major fuel, blood glucose. Where cerebral arteriosclerosis exists, brain-cell glucose deprivation can seriously hamper mental functioning.

Nicotine also encourages hypoglycemia by causing an increased release of adrenal hormones. These raise the level of glucose in the blood, stimulating a further release of insulin—and the hypoglycemic cycle is once again under way.

Investigators from the Philadelphia General Hospital Division of Cardiology report that heavy smoking causes a 27–77 percent rise in the blood level of the adrenal hormones. They documented a 64 percent rise in dogs and a 58 percent rise in rats when these experimental animals were injected with nicotine solution.

Dr. Omer Pelletier, a prominent Canadian researcher, has found that nicotine not only interferes with vitamin C absorption, it actually destroys some of the vitamin C already in the blood. A smoker must therefore take more than twice as much vitamin C to match a nonsmoker's ascorbic-acid blood levels.

In a test-tube experiment conducted at the University of Syracuse, researchers confirmed this by adding an amount of nicotine equal to that found in a heavy smoker's blood to a whole blood sample. One-third of the vitamin C in the sample was immediately destroyed.

Do you smoke because you are nervous, or are you nervous because you smoke?

Smoking and emotional difficulties are likely to keep each other going. British researchers have found that heavy smoking creates a desire for caffeine and sugar. Smokers drink far more coffee, heavily sugared, than nonsmokers; twice as many smokers have been found among drinkers than among nondrinkers. In combination, caffeine, nicotine, alcohol, and refined sugar put a tremendous strain on the body's ability to control blood-glucose levels, and emotional disturbances escalate in turn.

No smoker who has tried to quit needs to be told that nicotine is addictive. The average smoker requires nicotine not just daily but hourly. Nearly 80 percent of male smokers and more than 60 percent of female smokers consume fifteen or more cigarettes daily, or one cigarette per waking hour.

Dr. Hamilton Russell of the Addiction Research Unit of the British Institute of Psychiatry notes that the dependent smoker craves nicotine every thirty to sixty minutes. He has found through animal research that the pack-and-a-half-a-day smoking habit correlates with the need to maintain high nicotine levels in the brain.

Withdrawal symptoms characteristic of heavy smokers who try to quit match those found in other addictions: nervousness, drowsiness, anxiety, headaches, energy loss, sweating, cramps, tremors, and palpitations.

What kind of smoker are you? What do you get out of smoking? Are you hooked on nicotine?

The editors of the *Medical Bulletin on Tobacco* have compiled a list of statements made by smokers describing what they get out of cigarettes. How often do you feel this way when smoking? Mark your score after each statement: 5, always; 4, frequently; 3, occasionally; 2, seldom; 1, never.

A.   I smoke cigarettes to keep myself from slowing down.
B.   Handling a cigarette is part of the enjoyment of smoking.
C.   Smoking cigarettes is pleasant and relaxing.
D.   I light up when I feel angry about something.
E.   When out of cigarettes I find it almost unbearable until I can get them.
F.   I smoke automatically without even being aware of it.
G.   I smoke to stimulate me, to perk myself up.
H.   Part of the enjoyment comes from the steps I take to light up.
I.   I find cigarettes pleasurable.
J.   When I feel uncomfortable or upset, I light up.
K.   I am very aware of the fact when I am not smoking.
L.   I light up without realizing I still have one burning.
M.   I smoke cigarettes to give me a lift.
N.   Part of the enjoyment is watching the smoke.
O.   I want a cigarette most when comfortable, relaxed.
P.   When I feel blue, or want to take my mind off cares and worries, I smoke cigarettes.
Q.   I get a real gnawing hunger for a cigarette when I haven't smoked for a while.

R.   I've found a cigarette is in my mouth and didn't remember putting it there.

Insert your score on each question over its matching letter in the following factors. A total score of 11 or above is high; score of 7 or below is low.

Factor 1.   _____+_____+_____=_____
              A.   G.   M.   Stimulation
Factor 2.   _____+_____+_____=_____
              B.   H.   N.   Handling
Factor 3.   _____+_____+_____=_____
              C.   I.   O.   Relaxation
Factor 4.   _____+_____+_____=_____
              D.   J.   P.   Tension
Factor 5.   _____+_____+_____=_____
              E.   K.   Q.   Addiction
Factor 6.   _____+_____+_____=_____
              F.   L.   R.   Habit

Scoring 11 or higher on any factor indicates that it is an important source of satisfaction for you; the higher your score (15 is the highest), the more important is that particular factor. If you do not score high on *any* of the six factors, you either do not smoke very much or have not been smoking for very long. For you, giving up smoking should be easy. If you score high on several factors, you apparently get several kinds of satisfaction from smoking and will find it hard to stop.

The editors of the *Medical Bulletin on Tobacco* offer this interpretation of your test results:

Stimulation. If you score high on this factor, it means that you are one of those smokers who is stimulated by the cigarette—you feel that it helps wake you up, organize your energies, and keep you going. For you, physical activity could be a useful substitute.

Handling. Handling things can be satisfying, but there are many ways to keep your hands busy without lighting up or playing with a cigarette.

Relaxation. It is not always easy to find out whether you use the cigarettes to feel good—that is, get real, honest pleasure out of smoking (Factor 3)—or to keep from feeling bad (Factor 4). About two-thirds score high or fairly high on accentuation of pleasure, and about half of these also score as high or higher on reduction of negative feelings. Those who do get real pleasure out of smoking often find that an honest consideration of the harmful effects of their habit is enough to help them quit.

Tension. Many smokers use the cigarette as a kind of crutch in moments of stress or discomfort. But the heavy smoker, the person who tries to handle severe personal problems by smoking many times a day, is apt to discover that cigarettes do not effectively help him deal with tension. Again, physical activity may substitute.

Addiction. Quitting smoking is difficult for the person who scores high on this factor. For him the craving for the next cigarette begins to build up the moment he puts one out, so tapering off is not likely to work. He must go "cold turkey." It may be helpful for him to smoke more than usual for a day or two, so that the taste for cigarettes is spoiled, and then isolate himself completely from cigarettes until the craving is gone.

Habit. This kind of smoker is no longer getting much satisfaction from his cigarettes. He just lights them without even realizing he is doing so. The key to success is becoming aware of each cigarette you smoke.

"I can't quit smoking," a friend of ours complained one day. "I know I've tried and then can't work. I'd go broke if I stopped smoking."

John B., a forty-five-year-old medical writer, had smoked two packs a day for many years and knew he was endangering his health. He said, laughing, "Every new article I write about the terrible things smoking does to people makes me so nervous I light another cigarette. But when I try to stop, I can't function."

John was so nervous he not only smoked too much, he ate poorly. The combination created a nutrient-depleted state that left him particularly vulnerable to his addiction. We urged him to try vitamin supplementation and the Optimal Diet for one month as a way of cutting his smoking down.

It worked. John's still earning his living, but he's eating better and smoking less and less.

Would you like to lick your cigarette habit? Put away your "I Quit" button and try improving your diet. The Optimal Diet will help overcome your dependence on nicotine, will lessen your craving for cigarettes, and will neutralize some of the unpleasant side effects of withdrawal. If you suffer from circulatory or respiratory diseases, and cannot or will not give up smoking, megadoses of vitamin C, vitamin E, vitamin A, and vitamin B_3 together with the Optimal Diet will all combat the detrimental effects of nicotine.

Drug-created malnutrition and the mental disturbance that follows can result from doctor-prescribed drugs as easily as from those you take up on your own. Dr. Jean Mayer, professor of nutrition at Harvard, believes a vast number of people suffer from *iatrogenic* (doctor-caused) *malnutrition.*

Many psychiatrists automatically prescribe antipsychotic (psychotropic) drugs for their mentally disturbed patients. Often the nutrient deficiencies already responsible for the patient's emotional distress are only worsened, for the prescribed medicine actually incites further nutrient depletion. Antipsychotic medications may control the condition for which they were prescribed, but at great cost: they can interfere with nutrient metabolism and cause new mental abnormalities to appear.

Long-term or high-dosage therapy with the phenothiazines and other antipsychotic medications cause *tardive dyskinesia,* a disease characterized by rhythmical involuntary movements of the tongue, face, mouth, arms, or legs. The Food and Drug Administration has recommended that these medications be stopped immediately upon the appearance of such symptoms.

Drugs that depress the central nervous system sometimes intensify each other's effect, so that depression is actually increased rather than relieved. Such drugs include the barbiturates, other sedatives, tranquilizers, muscle relaxants, antihistamines, narcotic analgesics, pain relievers, and alcohol.

Although vitamin B_3 therapy is of great value in the treatment of mental illness, care must be exercised when antidepressants are also used: vitamin B_3 tends to enhance the effects of many drugs.

Drugs prescribed to cure physical diseases may cripple the mind. Indomethacin, used to treat arthritis, may cause psychiatric disturbances, epilepsy, and Parkinsonism. L-dopa, a popular treatment for Parkinson's disease, has been found to aggravate or to produce many neurological and psychotic symptoms. The drug can also induce a hypoglycemic reaction, a deficiency of vitamin B_6, and can increase oxygen consumption.

Where a single drug may not be harmful, the additive effects of two or more drugs may considerably impair the functioning of the brain. The combination of nonnarcotic analgesics or the common-pain relievers such as Darvon with some popular tranquilizers, for example, may cause tremors and mental confusion. The combination of a sedative with a nonprescription cold or allergy preparation containing an antihistamine can produce a similar reaction.

According to recent statistics, hospitalized patients may be taking an *average* of nine to thirteen drugs concurrently. Nonhospitalized, apparently healthy adults are estimated to be taking an average of three to four different drugs a day, by prescription or self-medication. In a recent survey, one-sixth of all hospital admissions were attributed to drug interactions or unintended reactions to therapeutic agents.

In hearings held before the United States Senate Subcommittee on Health in March of 1974, legislators heard a parade of witnesses testify that drug salesmen calling on doctors generally sidestep their obligation to inform physicians of the possible hazards of their products. Studies presented to the subcommittee indicated that more than half of the antibiotics used in hospitals across the country are either incorrectly prescribed or not needed at all. In short, the drug industry's aggressive marketing techniques and the resultant misuse of prescription drugs have led to deaths, disabilities, and mental ailments.

More than 35,000 prescription drugs are on the market, and new ones appear almost daily. No reliable source details the effects of one on the other, and doctors are understandably hard put to protect their patients. To make matters worse, the long list of warnings, contraindications, and possible adverse reactions, which must legally appear along with a drug's therapeutic claims, makes no mention of possible nutrient depletions resulting from its use.

The most glaring example of malnutrition by prescription occurs in women who take birth-contol pills *without supplementing their diet*. Oral contraceptives often cause widespread derangement of nutrient metabolism, and long-term use frequently results in some evidence of psychological upset. A number of scientific studies have shown mild to moderate depressions as well as symptoms of neurasthenia (lethargy, fatigue, insomnia, and restless sleep) to be the most common emotional response following reliance on the pill. New psychiatric symptoms or worsening of old ones occur in at least *one-half* of all pill users.

Why? At least four essential brain-cell nutrients are adversely affected: vitamin B_6, folic acid, vitamin B_{12}, and vitamin C.

Since B_6 metabolism is affected, 75 percent of all women on the pill do not properly utilize the essential amino acid, tryptophane. About fifty to a hundred times the normal body requirements of B_6 are needed to normalize tryptophane metabolism when oral contraceptives are taken. Women suffering the depression that B_6 depletion creates should either get off the pill or take a daily B_6 supplement (50-200 milligrams).

Oral contraceptives limit the absorption of the folic acid found in food, causing a low level of it in the blood. This deficiency cannot be corrected by eating more food. Only a folic-acid supplement will relieve the problem.

Oral contraceptives also lower blood levels of vitamin B_{12}, and so B_{12} supplementation (50-100 micrograms) is necessary for all pill users.

Finally, women on the pill can count on suffering low vitamin C concentrations in the blood. Oral contraceptives actually depress vitamin C levels and prevent the rise that normally takes place during ovulation. As much as one to two *grams* of vitamin C supplementation may be a daily necessity.

Is it any wonder that women on the pill experience a wide range of emotional symptoms? And these are compounded when medicine-cabinet potions are also taken, each of which in some small way may increase nutrient depletion.

Only a nutritionally oriented physician will alert you to deficiencies you may be suffering because of the drugs you are taking. Here's a check list you'd be well advised to keep handy when you're about to take any medication:

Medicine	Nutrient Deficiency Caused by the Medicine
analgesics (pain relievers)	
aspirin	vitamin C
antacids	vitamin B_1, calcium
antibiotics	vitamin K, most B vitamins
chloramphenicol	phenylalanine (essential amino acid)
isoniazid	vitamin B_6, other B vitamins
neomycin	vitamins A, B_{12}, D, E, and K
para-amino salicylic acid	vitamin B_{12}, folic acid
sulfonamides	folic acid and other B vitamins, vitamin K
tetracycline	calcium, pantothenic acid, vitamins C, B_6, and B_{12}

Medicine	Nutrient Deficiency Caused by the Medicine
blood-pressure-lowering agents	
hydralazines	vitamin B_6
cholesterol-lowering agents	vitamins A, D, E, and K
diuretics	
thiazides	potassium, vitamin C, and the B vitamins
hypoglycemic agents (oral)	vitamin B_{12}
laxatives	
mineral oil	vitamins A, D, E, and K
phenolphthalein	prevents absorption of many nutrients
sedative	
glutethimide	multiple vitamin deficiencies, especially vitamin D

Most people believe the nation's real drug problem to be our young people's use and abuse of chemical substances for mind-expanding experiments. Less well known are the promising results achieved in rehabilitating young drug addicts by nutritional therapy. In many cases juvenile drug abusers have been helped to break their habits and return to normal living once their internal chemical balance has been restored through diet and vitamin supplementation.

Nutritional improvement and megavitamin therapy with heavy doses of niacin and ascorbic acid has been reported to be particularly effective in combating LSD psychoses. The combination dramatically reduces postintoxication reactions and helps to bring addicts off their trips more easily. Maintenance on niacin therapy has effectively discouraged repeated abuses, particularly with those young addicts who have other nutritionally related disorders, such as hypoglycemia, allergies, and vitamin deficiencies. Such conditions are quite prevalent, especially if the drug abuser has been on the streets for any period of time.

A drug-abuse-prevention clinic in Arizona has adopted mega-vitamin therapy, using heavy doses of niacin and vitamin C to combat *drug wipeout syndrome*, a psychotic syndrome afflicting many who have taken legal and illegal drugs singly or in combination, with hallucinogenic effects.

The "drug wipeout" experience is a perceptual distortion, the feeling of being "stoned all the time." Drug wipeout afflicts at least several million present or former drug users, according to the Do It Now Foundation, a national organization involved with drug education. They believe this condition to be almost identical to borderline or early schizophrenia—and a deranged body metabolism to be at fault.

After four years of working with such cases, the foundation's Los Angeles branch has found that the megavitamin therapy we described for schizophrenia works equally well for their clients; doses of 3000–5000 milligrams *each* of vitamin C and niacin *daily* produce dramatic improvement in a very short period of time.

Withdrawal from barbiturate addiction can also be successfully counteracted with niacin and vitamin C. The Do It Now Foundation cautions, however, that withdrawal from barbiturates should *always* be done under the careful supervision of a doctor or medical clinic.

The foundation also recommends that niacin be considered by any doctor handling heroin withdrawal cases, both as a guarantee against convulsions and as postwithdrawal therapy. According to Vic Pawlak, the director, 85 percent of their cases recuperated following megavitamin treatment. Considering the low recovery rate of heroin addicts on other programs, that percentage borders on the astonishing.

Only a parent who has stood by helplessly, watching a son or daughter descend into the terrifying drug world, can appreciate the hopelessness that comes with the failure to reach, much less help, the child.

Belinda's parents knew that feeling all too well. Their daughter had run away from home at sixteen, lived first on the streets and then in one commune after another, and run the gamut of drug experimentation for more than a year. Occasionally she'd come back home, vowing to straighten out, but always something would trigger her return to her drug-using friends and her hapless, roving life.

When she came home for Christmas, her parents appealed to us. "Maybe you can talk some sense into her. She won't listen to us 'straights.' We don't know anything, according to Belinda."

She came to our office reluctantly, to say the least. We didn't make much progress until we began to talk about natural foods. Surprised to find a common ground, she said, "I'm really into organic eating. We're all onto the way food manufacturers are trying to poison us."

This slight wedge gave us the chance to get Belinda on the Optimal Diet, with heavy megadoses of niacin, ascorbic acid, and the other nutrients she needed. From time to time she'd come back to the office to "rap" about life. Each time she seemed a little brighter.

Belinda is back in school now. The terrible flashbacks from her drug-experimentation days rarely bother her any longer. Her biggest victory to date? She's convinced her parents to go on the Optimal Diet. "Dad's cut down his drinking, and Mom doesn't smoke as much as she used to," she reports. "They're a whole lot easier to live with, let me tell you."

Perhaps you now feel that America's drug problem has dimensions you may not have considered before. But remember, the everyday addict, who habitually uses caffeine, nicotine, or any of the many drugs mentioned, needs help along with the stereotyped addict hooked on illicit drugs.

Drugs and other chemical substances, regardless of the reason for their use, their legality or lack of it, are foreign to our molecular environment and invite emotional disaster when they enter the body. Malnutrition or metabolic disturbance is the ultimate result, and the remedy need be neither difficult nor complicated: good nutrition and vitamin supplementation can free you or someone you love from depending on drugs.

9

Problem-Solving:
The Psychodietetic Approach
to Sexual Inadequacy,
Hyperactivity, Senility, Allergy

Forty-seven-year-old Larry M. rarely skips his weekend golf. He's never broken ninety, but he's not discouraged. He feels defeated at home, though; his sex life is below par. "The old gal just doesn't turn me on anymore," he tells himself as he haunts neighborhood shops for books that might "up" his potency.

Thirty-three-year-old Marcia D. has three school-aged children. Two are "hyperactive" and must take calming drugs daily. Her husband thinks it's her fault. "Maybe my mother-in-law was right," she says. "I was never cut out to be a mother."

Mr. and Mrs. F. dread the future. Mr. F.'s widowed mother cannot live alone much longer. Last week she forgot the stove was on. Yesterday she got lost and a neighbor took her home. "Nursing homes aren't *that* bad," Mrs. F. has told her husband. "We can't bring her here to live, not the way she's been acting lately."

Twenty-nine-year-old Susan B. is afraid she's losing her mind. She often finds herself in tears and doesn't know why. She thinks her job might be to blame, though she used to enjoy it. Now she has crying jags even on weekends. Her group-therapy counselor, who thinks she ought to go back to school, has explained that her compulsive eating habits betray a lack of self-respect. Susan feels that no one understands. "Chocolate fudge sundaes," she says, "are the only thing I can *count on* to make me feel better."

These are ordinary people with an assortment of ordinary problems. What do they have in common? The fact that they can all be helped by the psychodietetic approach to problem solving. Unsatisfactory sexual relations, child-behavior difficulties, aging, and food-related "mental" illness are but a sampling of the many everyday conditions that yield to nutritional therapy.

Dietary "solutions" to sexual problems have been with us throughout history. The Book of Genesis recommends mandrake to stimulate potency and fertility; bird's-nest soup is among the numerous suggestions for would-be lovers to be found in ancient Oriental literature; and from Arabia comes repeated advice that desert sheiks consume large quantities of eggs, milk, and honey, along with nuts, sesame seeds, garlic, and onions, in order to keep their harems happy.

We know better today. Or do we?

No *one* food increases sexual capacity; yet the age-old concept of the aphrodisiac is not as scientifically invalid as you might think. Many of the foods lauded as passion-producing in ages past have subsequently been found to be an excellent source for minerals, vitamins, essential amino acids, and fatty acids necessary to the proper functioning of the sex glands.

Do oysters make you sexy? They contain zinc, without which the male gland cannot perform. Dr. James Leathem of the Bureau of Biological Research at Rutgers University has demonstrated that zinc and manganese are both indispensable to a healthy prostate and may help a degenerating gland to recover.

Vitamin E cannot guarantee sensuality, but it does stimulate the production and motility of the male sperm, and it helps prevent miscarriages and premature births when given to pregnant females. Vitamin E therapy has proved useful in cases of menopausal disturbance, through its calming effect on women facing "the change." Both men and women may feel more sexually vigorous when vitamin E is added to their diets, for as a cell-oxidizing agent with circulation-stimulating properties it increases general vitality, muscular stamina, and cardiac efficiency.

Every known nutrient can make some sexual claim. The bioflavonoids found in citrus fruits and juices, for example, have been used to bring dramatic relief from the "hot flashes" suffered by menopausal women. Nor can the B vitamins be overlooked. If they are in short supply, husbands and wives become predisposed to tensions that are certain to make them candidates for sexual inadequacy.

The "I'm too tired" syndrome that sexually disrupts so many marriages can be traced directly to overall nutritional deficiencies, which contribute to an underactive thyroid, which in turn leads to decreased libido and chronic fatigue.

Male impotence is no longer a complaint limited to the gray-haired. Its increased incidence among the young is more likely to be the result of the increased incidence of hypoglycemia than a fear-reaction to sexually active feminists (a favorite claim of male psychiatrists). At the Tel Aviv Medical School in Israel, doctors who have investigated abnormal carbohydrate metabolism found that it contributed to male impotence at *every* age.

The fact of the matter is that sexual activity, one of mankind's most sensitive and easily disturbed bodily functions, is extraordinarily vulnerable to poor eating habits.

That correcting the diet can solve difficulties has been demonstrated time and again. Dr. Alfred G. Churchill, vice-president of the International Academy of Metabology, is an old-fashioned general practitioner up-to-the-minute in his knowledge of nutrition. "I'm certainly *not* a sex therapist," he says; yet he has a file full of case histories of patients restored to sexual vigor as a "side effect" of his cure-by-diet approach to medicine.

Mr. P., an overweight man in his fifties, was a typical case. Heavily involved with a challenging business, he ate out most of the time and at odd hours. He came to Dr. Churchill with many complaints, among which was loss of virility and sex drive.

An examination showed Mr. P. to be nutrient-deficient, hypoglycemic, and prediabetic. All three conditions were affecting his potency and making him a hard-to-live-with husband. Dr. Churchill's treatment included a "high-virility diet" comprising nutrient-rich foods and vitamin-mineral supplements. Mr. P. soon began to improve, only to suffer a new shock. His wife, a much younger woman, decided to enjoy an extended visit with her family in Europe. Mr. P. was afraid she might not return.

The additional emotional stress, which could have triggered a setback, did not. Mr. P. stuck to his nutritional regime, and when he welcomed his wife home six months later, he was a new man in every respect. At last report, they were living happily together.

Another of Dr. Churchill's patients—forty-one years old, yet already menopausal, felt, looked, and acted like a woman fifteen years older. On her first visit, she confessed she hadn't "had sex" with her husband for several years; she never felt "quite up to it," and in any case he was an impossible man who expected too much of her.

Dr. Churchill realized he had an impatient patient on his hands, one who would not cooperate for long without visible results. She had been living on an assortment of strong tranquilizers and sedatives for years, and her condition was further aggravated by menstrual distress. Hardly receptive to his suggestion that diet and vitamins could help her "at her age," as she put it, she nonetheless agreed to try his regimen. Dr. Churchill devised a crash program for her: a high-protein, low-carbohydrate, moderate-fat diet which emphasized fresh foods, liver, yogurt, and sesame seeds. A rapid response was insured by hormone and vitamin-mineral supplementation, with a heavy concentration of the B-complex vitamins.

Within two weeks she admitted that she felt like a "real woman" for the first time in her life and that her friends were accusing her of having had a face lift.

Ask Dr. Churchill for his most rewarding case, and he'll point to a photograph on his desk. "That's Mrs. T.'s *second* baby," he says, and then explains why the smiling infant in the picture represents such a victory.

Mrs. T.'s case dramatically illustrates what can happen when the stress of childbearing is thrust upon a metabolically weakened young woman. After her first pregnancy, this patient broke down completely. Her file describes a "twenty-three-year-old mess": she weighed less than a hundred pounds, was extremely depressed, cried frequently, was overcome with irrational fears, insecure, nervous, and given to emotional outbursts. Unable to care properly for her infant daughter, she was so desperately determined never to have another child that she had moved into the nursery rather than sleep with her husband.

In this extreme case, it took two years of proper diet, vitamin-mineral supplementation, and adrenal cortical extracts to bring the patient back to full emotional health; but Mrs. T. eventually underwent a second pregnancy with no difficulty and the happiest of results: a well-developed unusually alert baby joyfully welcomed into the world by its mother.

Sometimes children save marriages; more frequently, they break them up. It's no secret that family harmony dissolves when a child's disruptive behavior adds one discordant note atop another. In a monotonous round, mother blames father, who reciprocates in kind.

Parents who have uncritically accepted responsibility for the destructive behavior of their children can at last take heart. Malnutrition rather than psychological mishandling is proving again and again to be the true explanation as to why "difficult" children behave the way they do.

Dr. Bernard Rimland, director of the Institute for Child Behavior Research, has led the fight against child specialists who fault the mother for any problem the child may have. "Tell the charlatan to drop dead," is Dr. Rimland's advice to mothers with heavy hearts who have been blamed by some professional for their child's learning disorders, violence, or autism. His nationwide studies on the use of megavitamin therapy for a variety of behavior difficulties have produced impressive results, supporting his belief that a biochemical abnormality underlies many childhood disorders.

Three hundred children participated in one of Dr. Rimland's

programs. They were all "special" children inasmuch as either their parents, teachers, or guardians had found them to be extremely hard to handle, abnormally aggressive, or unresponsive to attempts at establishing normal controls.

He and his staff designed a special vitamin formula for these children: from 2 to 3 grams a day each of vitamins C and B_3 (in the form of niacinamide); 150–450 milligrams of vitamin B_6; 200 milligrams of pantothenic acid; plus a high-potency B-complex tablet. A unique feature of the project made it impossible for Dr. Rimland to influence the results in any way. The children, who lived in communities spread across the country, were all under local medical supervision. Their own doctors, not Dr. Rimland, evaluated their responses to treatment.

Both parents and physicians were asked to keep detailed records of the children's behavior patterns: sleep, speech, hearing, tantrums, alertness, cooperativeness, and other general and specific demeanor. At the end of the testing period, independent judges helped evaluate the computerized data. The final scoring showed that well over 50 percent of the children on the program had improved significantly.

Proud of his results but worried about the children who did *not* respond, Dr. Rimland speculated that there were undetected nutrient needs, possibly of a genetic origin, in the unimproved patients. For one such case he tried a double dose of vitamin B_6, and the mother reported an immediate difference: "She is eager to do things—a slight suggestion and she's ready for almost anything . . . she hasn't printed her name or numbers for over a year, but she's doing it now. I can't emphasize enough how she has refused to do anything these past months. Even my husband, who is a disbeliever, says she has improved these past four days."

The pioneer researcher in megavitamin therapy for disturbed children is Dr. Alan Cott, who has traveled to Russia to study fasting regimens and vitamin programs. His treatment for hyperactive children and for children with learning disabilities duplicates the approach (essentially Rimland's) he has found successful in youthful cases of schizophrenia. It now includes dosages of vitamin B_{15} (pangamic acid), which the Russians have found promising in their treatment of mental retardation. B_{15} has not yet been seriously investigated in the United States, but Soviet scientists believe that it aids in the respiration of brain tissue.

Dr. Abram Hoffer believes both the hyperactive child and the poor learner to be suffering a niacin deficiency. He treated one seven-year-old whose irrational fears had reached the point where he refused to take a bath, convinced that he would drown. A daily dose of 1.5 grams of nicotinamide (a form of vitamin B_3), plus a daily megadose of vitamin C, brought the child back to normal within seven months.

What is a healthy normal child like? Active, lively, bursting with energy. But if a child is a constant jumping jack, so filled with get-up-and-go that everyone who meets him wishes he were somewhere else, then he is today's hyperkinetic, or hyperactive, case.

Hyperkinesis is a relatively new medical term describing a clinical condition now diagnosed in more than 5 percent of American grade-school children. In some school districts the estimate runs as high as *25 to 40 percent.*

The hyperkinetic or hyperactive child is not merely "nervous"; he is unable to sit still for a minute. He has such a short attention span that he learns little. Easily irritated, he is so aggressive and disruptive that he's a schoolroom catastrophe.

Dr. Ben Feingold, a California allergy specialist who has carefully researched the condition, attributes it directly to diet, specifically, an allergic brain reaction to a group of chemicals called salicylates. These chemicals are to be found in the flavoring and coloring agents (there are over 3,000 of them) commonly used in "convenience" foods that are the mainstay of most children's diets.

The average child gets a highly poisonous daily dose of salicylates. He starts the day with a loaded breakfast cereal, and by bedtime he has swallowed untold amounts of soft drinks, fruit ades, chocolate beverages, hot dogs, luncheon meats, ice cream—a long, monotonous list of familiar offenders. A conscientious mother unwittingly provides an extra dose when the daily vitamin pill she gives her child is a brand that has been gussied up for kids.

Dr. Feingold has duplicated a Dr. Jekyll–Mr. Hyde scenario by altering children's diets either to include or to eliminate the additives. When artificially colored and flavored foods were restricted, 60 percent of his patients quieted down practically overnight. Allowed back on such foods, they became hyperactive once more.

Miniscule amounts of offending substances can drastically alter a child's behavior. This is not surprising, when you consider that the child's central nervous system is far more susceptible to insult than is the average adult's. The resulting problems can be corrected as easily as switching a light from "on" to "off," once the cause is understood.

The younger the child, the more vulnerable. A few years ago a group of healthy infants at the Massachusetts Institute of Technology proved just *how* vulnerable when they suddenly began acting quite erratically; some even had convulsions. Dr. Coursin, the pediatrician in charge, began an investigation and discovered that batches of nursery-prepared formula had been accidentally overheated, so much so that the vitamin B_6 content had been destroyed. He ordered immediate vitamin supplementation. In a matter of minutes the infants improved, and their symptoms soon disappeared entirely.

Such an incident points up the importance of having *all* nutrients *constantly* available. The younger the child, the more bizarre the reaction when diet is not what it should be.

Research on lower animals has confirmed, in study after study, that nutritional deprivation has a negative effect on both behavior and learning capacity. The collective results are impressive and indicate that, if scientists were ruthless enough to repeat these experiments using human subjects, the effects would be similar. Parents are not likely to expose their offspring to nutritional deprivation in the name of science; yet they unwittingly do so through ignorance.

Dr. Merrill S. Read, director of the Growth and Development Branch of the National Institute of Child Health and Development, has devoted his life to the study of how nutrition affects children. Among his findings:

Children who are apathetic, unable to pay attention, and disruptive in the classroom very often are those who attend classes without having had any breakfast.

Children identified as "nervous" by their teachers and showing no clinical signs of malnutrition improve noticeably after a midmorning snack of milk plus a calcium supplement.

Children can show a positive response to minimal efforts at nutritional improvement. In one experiment conducted in a university nursery, children from two to five were divided into two groups. Half received a midmorning fruit juice snack while the other half had plain water. Their behavior patterns were observed by trained investigators, who found that the midmorning fruit juice helped relieve fatigue and reduce irritability and other forms of negative behavior.

Only one school to our knowledge has put intensive nutritional therapy into practice. The Richard Forrest School in West Virginia, founded by Eunice Moss, specializes in problem children, many of whom have learning disorders as well as personality defects. The highly successful program there emphasizes correcting the students' diets. In one case, a six-year-old who came under Mrs. Moss's supervision was overweight, ill-tempered, unable to recognize the letters of the alphabet, and addicted to ice cream, hamburgers, and French fries. Two years on the school's regimen changed him into a star pupil who reads far better than others his age and has an engaging, outgoing personality.

In Dallas, young patients are specifically referred to pediatrician Dr. Hugh L. Powers, Jr., when they have failed to progress in school as well as had been expected.

Dr. Powers has rarely found teaching inadequacies to blame.

His treatment, prescribed after a complete medical work-up, varies from patient to patient. Certain basics, however, apply to all:

Limitation of carbohydrates and exclusion of coffee, sugar, tea, and cola drinks.

Digestive enzymes to enhance use of protein as a source of glucose.

A concentrated vitamin B and C supplement.

Dr. Powers does not promise straight-A report cards, but the performance of virtually all patients who follow his regimen improves.

From childhood to old age is not the quantum leap it may seem. Only the very young believe aging happens only to "other people."

"I don't mind growing old, I just don't want to end up senile." Sound familiar? Contrary to popular wisdom, senility (poor memory, confusion, irrational thinking, short temper) is a *disease*, not an inevitable condition. There are people over a hundred who are not senile, while some are senile at forty-five or fifty.

A cluster of symptoms masquerades under the name of "senility." Most of them—loss of appetite, fatigue, irritability, anxiety, depression, inability to remember recent events, insomnia, distractibility, and mild delusional states—go hand in hand with general and specific dietary deficiency.

In the elderly who are senile, many brain cells have been lost. Those that are left get just enough oxygen and nutrients to remain alive, but not enough to remain functionally effective. These oxygen-starved cells *can be rescued*, if treated properly and in time. Dr. Edwin Boyle, Jr., research director of the Miami Heart Institute, has corrected the memory loss associated with senility by placing patients in a closed chamber where they breathe pure oxygen at three times the normal atmospheric pressure. This forces oxygen to the brain and brings immediate benefit, especially where cerebral arteriosclerosis (narrowing and hardening of the blood vessels supplying the brain) is present.

Patients regain the ability to recall recent events; they can once again process new information. The improvement lasts from six weeks to six months after a single treatment.

Oxygen-starved brain cells can also be the result of oxidation, a chemical reaction in the blood between oxygen and other substances. This can be prevented in large measure by the antioxidant vitamins: vitamin C, vitamin E, and vitamin A.

Niacin can also enhance the oxidation of brain cells. It thins the blood by preventing "sludging," a clumping together of blood cells that interferes with circulation. Vitamin E decreases the oxygen requirements of the tissues, particularly muscles, and the oxygen thus saved is passed on to brain cells.

At the Missouri Institute of Psychiatry, researchers have found that the addition of B-complex vitamins and vitamin C to the diet of geriatric patients causes a dramatic reduction of "excitability." The daily supplement contained 15 milligrams of thiamine, 10 milligrams of riboflavin, 5 milligrams of pyridoxine, 50 milligrams of niacinamide, 10 milligrams of pantothenic acid, and 300 milligrams of ascorbid acid. These patients, all of whom were on tranquilizers, calmed down only after the multiple-vitamin supplement was added to their treatment program.

At Nether Edge Hospital and at Winter Street Hospital in Sheffield, England, senility is treated as simple malnutrition. Dr. M. L. Mitra has found that the elderly suffer more severely from faulty diet than does any other age group. They require larger amounts of basic nutrients to counteract the effects of both disease and a variety of prescribed medications that interfere with vitamin metabolism. In many of Dr. Mitra's cases, mental confusion and disoriented behavior either diminished or disappeared following the appropriate vitamin therapy: vitamin B complex and vitamin C.

Dr. Hoffer puts the chronic malnutrition now mislabeled as "senility" into a new category of deficiency diseases, which he terms *acquired dependency disease* and defines as "the condition in which the patient requires substantially larger quantities of a particular vitamin than the average person, even on the order of perhaps a thousand times as much."

Dr. Hoffer says that for many years scientists have known that there is a time limit to normal recovery from nutritional deficiency, although the limit is ill-defined. If the vitamin deficiency has been present longer than the period of time in which recovery is possible, there is no response to supplementation in the usual dosage range. In such a case, megadoses are required to restore and maintain health.

Many elderly persons have been deprived of essential nutrients for long periods of time. Their body requirements can no longer be met by nutrients obtained from food, and they suffer mental deterioration. Like rain-starved plants, they need saturation treatment, and this means megadoses of all essential elements. Dr. Hoffer's recommended therapy is a result of trial and error. He added and combined increasing doses of several nutrients until he got the desired response. He now advises trying the following, in order: nicotinic acid, pyridoxine, ascorbic acid, vitamin B_{12}, vitamin E, and *l*-glutamine, with some vitamin A and D.

Dr. Hoffer has close-to-home proof that his methods can reverse as well as prevent senility. Twenty years ago, when his mother was sixty-seven years old, she was suffering many of the degenerative ailments normally considered to be chronic and hopeless in the aging. She was nervous and depressed, complained of severe pain in her joints, failing vision in one eye, generalized weakness and fatigue, and severe arthritis of her hands, Dr. Hoffer has reported. Most disturbing of all, "her memory was beginning to fail. It was clear she was aging very quickly."

At the time, Dr. Hoffer's megavitamin therapy was still in the theoretical stage, and he began giving his mother 3 grams of nicotinic acid a day just to be "doing something." Six weeks later, to his surprise, his mother's arthritis had cleared, the vision in both eyes was normal, her tension, anxiety, and depression were gone.

Over the years she remained in good health, and now, at

eighty-seven, she is physically weaker, but mentally intact, well enough to have nursed Dr. Hoffer's father through terminal cancer and to have coauthored a book dealing with her pioneer days as a homesteader. Mrs. Hoffer is currently at work on her memoirs, which may well serve as a testimonial to her son's treatment for the "incurable" disease of senility.

Although there is no stopping the clock or turning back the calendar, you can inoculate yourself against the distressing symptoms of senility by paying close attention to nutrition all the years along the way to the eighties and nineties. And for those who have an "Uncle Charlie" in the family, an aging relative who seems day by day to be losing his marbles, giving him carefully chosen vitamin-mineral supplements could prove far more beneficial to all concerned than a search for a good nursing home.

Of all the eccentric relationships that have been found between food and mental performance, those uncovered by Dr. Marshall Mandell may well be the most startling. Having designated himself as a "clinical ecologist," he is in the vanguard of a brand-new science exploring the premise that much mental illness is actually food allergy in disguise.

Ecological mental illness (EMI) is Dr. Mandell's term to describe hypersensitivity to natural and synthetic substances in food, water, and air. He considers EMI to be a common ailment that is more often misdiagnosed and incorrectly treated than not.

Over two hundred of his patients to date have been relieved of long-standing emotional complaints once specific allergens were removed from their diets. Most had no idea that an allergy might be responsible for their problems before they were tested from this viewpoint. The majority had been to at least one psychiatrist who had blamed emotional stress for their ailments.

The complex nature of EMI requires exhaustive testing before allergens can be pinpointed. In one case, that of a forty-year-old man with a history of chronic fatigue, mental confusion, and nervous tension, previously diagnosed as psychosomatic, fifteen food tests were given. The results showed that after eating wheat the patient became restless, tense, and unable to concentrate; that coffee made him lightheaded and gave him a headache; that chicken produced a "nervous" reaction characterized by dizziness and confusion; that eggs made him yawn and unable to concentrate; that peas brought on a tired, headachy, flushed feeling; that corn made him tense and irritable.

No medication or allergy treatments were necessary. He simply avoids eating the major test-incriminated foods and restricts his intake of the minor offenders. He has been well for over a year.

Dr. Mandell found a young working mother complaining of nightly fatigue, depression, and irritability to be allergic to potatoes, which made her "feel peculiar"; to tea, which gave her headaches; to milk, which made her restless; and to wheat, which brought on nausea and head pains. This patient had always eaten a bowl of cold wheat cereal with milk when she returned from work at ten o'clock each evening. By ten fifteen she would be unhappy and irritable, yet she never associated the two events. She had discussed her problems with her minister and her family physician, both of whom had assured her that the bitter arguments she had with her husband every night were due to the physical and emotional stress of her very long day, which included household duties, the care of four children, and a part-time job. She had continually been urged to give up the job.

Instead, after being tested, she gave up her nightly minimeal, with the result that her irritability, fatigue, and depression disappeared.

One of Dr. Mandell's most misunderstood patients was an eight-year-old boy who performed so badly at school, often falling asleep at his desk late in the day, that his teachers predictably classified him as a nonachiever and a hopeless daydreamer.

Not hopeless at all, Dr. Mandell discovered. On investigation, chocolate-flavored foods were found to be a prominent feature of the school's lunch menu. The boy always chose chocolate milk and chocolate ice cream and snacked on chocolate cupcakes or chocolate-chip cookies. He was also exceptionally fond of an oat-flour breakfast cereal and had at least two bowls before starting his school day.

Oats and chocolate proved to be the boy's two major allergies. He stopped eating both and stopped having difficulties in school.

This boy's experience illustrates an important aspect of EMI: *chronic food addiction.* Dr. Mandell has found that allergy victims often crave their poison. They overeat the very substances that are the offenders, because these make them feel better temporarily.

Like a heroin addict who suffers withdrawal symptoms when the drug is too long absent, allergic patients experience discomfort when they do not get the foods to which they are addicted. They feel relief after they eat the allergen, and, unknowingly, perpetuate the cycle.

Dr. Mandell considers alcoholism and obesity to represent the maximum development of such a cycle. The overweight person who "must" have chocolate, who has an irresistible urge to raid the icebox at night, who inevitably wolfs down the taboo items on his diet, is much like the alcoholic who has to have a drink no matter what the consequences. Both could be treated with new understanding if their eating and drinking patterns were identified as classic withdrawal symptoms.

Schizophrenia is being reexamined in light of Dr. Mandell's findings. In a random sampling of 56 hospitalized patients, 92.2 percent were found to be allergic to at least one or more common substances, and when Dr. Mandell tested a group of patients diagnosed as hard-to-treat neurotics unresponsive to the usual psychotherapeutic techniques, he found that 88 percent of them were allergic to wheat, 50 percent to corn, and 60 percent to milk.

Dr. Mandell's video-taped recordings of patients in the throes of "mental" reactions to injections of offending foods include a man crying when given corn, a woman turning "mean" after chocolate, another woman grimacing and squirming from green peppers, a man leaping from his chair and thrashing about from oranges. His work is still in the exploratory stage, but it offers hope that a great many common emotional problems are reversible biochemical dysfunctions.

We have found that some allergic reactions are either caused or intensified by hypoglycemia. Little or no allergic reaction may be found to an offending food or chemical when blood-sugar level is normal, but the same substance will produce a strong response when blood sugar is low. Allergies compounded by hypoglycemia are significantly reduced when the hypoglycemic diet is followed.

What can you do if you suspect that an undiscovered allergy lies at the heart of your difficulties?

If possible, you should seek the help of an allergy specialist. Most larger cities have professionals experienced in administering the tests necessary to determine which substances, or combinations of substances, are aggravating.

If the advice of a specialist is hard to come by, you might turn to prominent allergist Dr. Arthur F. Coca. Having discovered that the pulse quickens after the ingestion of foods to which one is allergic, he has written a book, *The Pulse Test*, which can help you uncover your own allergies (see Appendix B).

Here is an abbreviated outline of the test:

1. Keep a detailed record of *everything* you eat for seven days.
2. Take your pulse several times a day during this week: before rising, just before each meal, thirty minutes after each meal, and just before bedtime. If you never get a pulse count over 84, you probably do not have an allergy. A pulse count higher than 85 probably indicates that some food you have eaten is producing an allergic reaction. If there is a variance during the day, or more than a two-beat variance from day to day, you are definitely allergic. If your pulse rate fluctuates in such a way as to indicate that you are allergic one day but not another, repeat the diet eaten on the suspicious day and see what happens.
3. Smoking complicates the picture. Give up cigarettes while testing yourself for an allergy.

If you have decided you're allergic to something and want to find out what it is, you'll have to devote some weekends to narrowing down the allergens. Eat nothing Friday night; Saturday morning, take your pulse before eating *just one* of the foods you ordinarily eat, then take it again after eating this single food. Repeat this procedure at two-hour intervals. Several weekends may be necessary before you have found the one or more substances causing your pulse to rise. Eliminate them from your diet, and you'll quite possibly eliminate some if not all of your "emotional" symptoms.

No self-test summarizes this chapter. We doubt that any is needed. You are probably all too aware of your problems. The common ones we have discussed here are meant to be indicative of the *many* ways in which a change in diet can either resolve one of life's difficulties, or ease the condition so that it no longer seems too overwhelming to handle.

Many thousands of people have found new hope when they learned that their diets were responsible for their troubles. Longstanding metabolic disorders are frequently corrected in a matter of months, ending years of suffering and confusion. The psychodietetic approach is valuable not just for the seriously disturbed but for everyone facing the ordinary difficulties of life.

Problems? Everyone has them.

Solutions? Closer to hand than you may have believed.

Changing your diet can change your life. You don't have to take our word for it; you can prove it for yourself.

10
Hidden Nondietary Factors That Influence Emotions

"You nutritionists think you have all the answers! You mean to tell me nothing but diet affects the way people feel?"

Not at all. We are well aware that a multitude of factors determine the way people function. An exhaustive search of all contributing forces would fill a library, and many might still be overlooked. Psychiatrists, psychologists, sociologists, anthropologists, social historians, religionists, educators, and economists have all unearthed behavioral influences.

Food nonetheless remains *the* key, inasmuch as optimal nutrition increases the ability to combat other influences. Our exploration of "hidden" stresses that have attracted very little attention points up how much is yet unknown about the many sources of emotional distress.

Take "silent sounds," for example. You can't hear them, but they influence you nonetheless.

Hundreds of studies have documented the detrimental effects of "real" noise on your psyche. If you work in a steel factory, or live near an airport, beside a heavily trafficked highway, with a drum-playing teen-ager, you don't need a scientist to tell you that "noise pollution" is nerve-shattering.

But what about the sounds you cannot hear?

Very low-frequency sounds, below the 20 Hertz level and generally inaudible to the human ear, are known as *infrasounds*. These "silent sounds" come from many sources, some natural, others man-made. Earthquakes, hurricanes, major storms, volcanic eruptions send low-level waves thousands of miles from the source. Missile launchings, construction machinery, explosions, defective electric motors, and aircraft also produce infrasonics. Previously these were assumed to be inconsequential; recent research has uncovered the strange effects they have on people.

In 1968 Dr. Floyd Dunn, a professor of engineering at the University of Illinois, found that auto accidents and school absenteeism rose to abnormal highs in Chicago on days of heavy infrasonic activity. Insurance-company records and school-attendance figures provided the statistics. During the three-week survey period, sophisticated monitoring equipment showed the area to be under bombardment by heavy infrasonic activity. Dr. Dunn concluded that the city-wide deviation from normal behavior could only be attributed to the "silent sounds."

John Green, a Bell Telephone electrical engineer, reports that infrasonics can easily disrupt people's work habits. When a local company's staff reacted badly after they were moved to new, modern, more comfortable quarters, he was called in to investigate.

Previously a cooperative and genial group, the employees now were edgy and quarrelsome. Absenteeism was running high, morale was low. Company executives could find no reason for the constant bickering and petty jealousies. The trouble was traced to an improperly installed air-conditioning unit that was emitting infrasonics. Once the unit was fixed, the employees' behavior returned to normal.

NASA researchers learned to take "silent sounds" seriously when they found that the infrasonics surrounding the launch platform during the first three minutes of a space probe seriously impaired the astronauts' ability to do mathematical calculations, or translate verbal instructions, accurately.

Military experts in many countries consider infrasonics a possible weapon, and police departments have investigated their potential as a "painless" method of riot control. Secret service officials have proposed infrasonically bombarded interrogation chambers for uncooperative witnesses. Such applications of infrasonics are feasible, since people exposed to the sounds become docile, confused, and vulnerable to suggestion.

French researchers have found that volunteers subjected to infrasonics become sleepy, anxious, headachy, and disoriented.

How may "silent sounds" be affecting you? Tests have shown that a car traveling at sixty miles per hour produces infrasonics sufficient to disturb the driver. This is a possible explanation for many mysterious single-car highway accidents.

One group of distinguished scientists recently suggested that infrasonics can cause sane people to "act crazy." In one case a woman threatened suicide because of noises only she could hear. A tape recording verified that she was reacting to infrasonic background noises. Many mental patients undergoing treatment because they "hear things" may be exhibiting a heightened sensitivity to silent sounds.

One authority, having found evidence of senseless murders committed at the exact time weather bureau reports showed severe storm-generated infrasonics in the vicinity, believes these silent sounds can trigger insanity in borderline cases. He had discovered numerous instances where abnormal behavior erupted during periods of high winds and storms, both infrasonic generators.

Some people are obviously more vulnerable than others, and while "silent sounds" usually cannot be avoided, an optimal state of nutrition *will* help inoculate you against their effects.

The "odorless fumes" of our polluted atmosphere, just as hard to escape as infrasounds, have also been found responsible for a wide range of mental disturbances, from "butterflies in the stomach" to paranoid delusions. During hot, humid, high-pollution days, patient suffering from nonspecific air-pollution syndrome (NAPS) experience anxiety, are distrustful, tremorous, and may even find themselves sexually inadequate.

Clean-air advocates are generally concerned with heart, lung, and respiratory ills brought about by pollution. They tend to overlook the dangers of mental functioning.

A recent donnybrook in the District of Columbia erupted when an incinerator's mercury emissions were found to be 40 percent higher than federal law allows. A top government expert did not consider the emissions a "serious health hazard"; yet psychiatrists have reported that mercury inhalation causes children to become irritable, hostile, and seriously depressed.

You need not live in a high-pollution area to suffer mental disturbances from odorless fumes. A variety of common household products can cause emotional upset. The case files of Dr. Mandell, the allergist mentioned earlier, include housewives made irrational by their natural-gas ovens, hair sprays, disinfectants, cleaning materials, wall paint, floor wax, and insecticides. As more and more chemicals and products made from chemicals (such as plastics) come into use, we find more complaints of headaches, mood swings, crying jags, bad dreams, and so on. Seemingly innocuous items, from permanent-press garments to plastic-backed carpeting, have been found to trigger the complaints. Dr. Mandell had one patient who always wept on washdays: not because she found doing the laundry distasteful, but because the chlorine bleach she used caused an emotional reaction. Many housewives who are constantly depressed and overtired assume the cause to be overwork or nerves, but they could be experiencing a sensitivity to chemical fumes.

Allergy experts advise a thorough airing of the home periodically and careful avoidance of suspected chemicals. If you live or work in a polluted area, take a clean-air break in the country whenever possible.

Sounds. Fumes. What else?

Light.

Some of the most interesting research of environmental influences and their effect on emotions has been done by Dr. John Nash Ott, a pioneer investigator into the effects of natural and artificial light on man, animals, and plants. He finds that our neon-lit society distorts brain and nervous-system functioning.

People working under pink fluorescent lights for only a few months tend to become tense and irritable. In a series of controlled animal experiments, Dr. Ott duplicated this effect by subjecting minks to pink lights. The animals turned "vicious." When he exposed them to sunlight filtered through deep blue plastic, their behavior was reversed, and they became "docile and friendly," abnormally so for minks.

His most recent finding is that student hyperactivity can be the result of fluorescently lit classrooms. Working with the Sarasota, Florida, County School Board, Dr. Ott used time-lapse photography to record the comparative effects of normal fluorescent lighting and full-spectrum lighting on student behavior. Under normal fluorescent lights, students were frequently tired, irritable, inattentive, and unruly. Once full-spectrum lights were substituted, they settled down; they paid more attention to their teachers, showed more interest in their studies, and rarely needed disciplining.

Parents concerned about their teen-agers' apathy and lack of ambition might well suspect the popular craze for strobe lights, which flicker and flash in time to high-decibel rock music. According to recent studies, about one-quarter of the population feels strange (giddy, dizzy, drunk, weak) when exposed to rapidly flashing lights. A major police and military equipment company is developing a "photic driver," a modified version of strobe lights, as a nonviolent crowd-control weapon. The device is silent and invisible, combining "silent sound" and infrared pulsations. Not surprisingly, it effectively subdues those who are subjected to it.

Few investigations to date have researched the psychological effects of humans deprived of natural light, but, in research with animals, rats turned to alcohol solutions rather than plain drinking water when kept in total darkness for two weeks. Seventy-five percent went back to plain water once normal laboratory lighting conditions were restored.

Dr. Irving Geller has a biochemical explanation for this change in taste: when kept in darkness, the rat's pineal gland produces more melatonin and a melatonin-forming enzyme, *hydroxy-o-methyl transferase*. He has been able to make rats alcoholic merely by injecting them with a melatonin solution.

Every enzyme system depends on the combined action of an

apoenzyme, made primarily of amino acids, and a coenzyme, which usually includes a vitamin and/or a mineral element. Every nutrient swallowed is acted on by at least one enzyme system. An increase of melatonin-forming enzymes undoubtedly insults the nutritional mechanisms that balance the brain and nervous system.

Do dimly lit cocktail lounges provide atmosphere, or do they also up their customers' bar bills? Their darkened interiors may be increasing melatonin production, insuring alcoholic thirst.

How much mental distress can we blame on our artificially lit environment? No one knows, but many of us move about like moles, moving from artificially lit homes to fluorescent-lit work areas to neon-lit underground shopping centers. We drive in cars "protected" by tinted windshields and don sunglasses whenever we venture out of doors.

Full-spectrum lights, designed to approximate natural daylight, are now on the market. They do not produce enough ultraviolet rays to make your skin red or cause it to tan, but do provide health-giving effects. They are so effective that plant-lovers buy them to induce better growth and healthier foliage in light-deprived house plants. Light-deprived people surely deserve equal care.

Clear glasslike tinted plastics that do not screen out health-giving ultraviolet rays are available for eyeglasses and windows. For added protection, spend some time each day outdoors.

Artificial light, silent sounds, odorless fumes. Short of completely disrupting your life style, what can you do to offset such subtle but malevolent influences?

The answer: optimal nutrition as armor against *all* forms of stress, known and unknown. In this chapter we've been discussing comparatively innocuous environmental forces; the most deadly force, of course, is radiation. When radiation therapy is medically prescribed, the target disease must be severe indeed to warrant drastic bombardment.

Enter cancer. No one would deny that malignant growths within the body are evidence of the breakdown of its resistance to disease-causing factors. But even in the case of a disease as serious as cancer, providing the body with a superabundant supply of all essential nutrients will not only help to ward off external attacks but also increases chances of recovery after radiation therapy.

We proved this conclusively in 1966, by dramatically improving the rate of response in a group of cancer patients subjected to a radiation therapy with just one week of the psychodietetic approach—the Optimal Diet and nutrient supplementation.

The experimental group was made up of 54 female patients with biopsy-proven cervical cancer, all scheduled for radiation therapy at the Tumor Clinic in the University of Alabama Medical Center. One week prior to the start of radiation treatments, half the patients were placed on a diet high in protein, low in refined carbohydrates, and supplemented by a vitamin-mineral preparation potent enough to insure an excess of essential nutrients. The other twenty-seven women, given neither dietary counsel nor supplements, served as a control group.

Approximately three weeks after the termination of radiation therapy, the response of the two groups was compared. The control group showed an average radiation response of 63.3, normal for such treatment according to previous hospital records, with patient response ranging in degree from 0 to 100. Forty percent of the group displayed unfavorable scores; thus their prognosis was very poor.

In contrast, the experimental group averaged a 97.5 response. Scores ranged from a low of 91 to a high of 100; *every* patient showed a favorable response to the therapy, thus a good chance for survival.

If *one week* of "supernutrition" can affect cancer recovery in such a spectacular fashion, your best defense against any kind of stress—environmental, psychological, physical—is obvious: keep your nutritional status as high as you possibly can.

Just as nutrition has generally been overlooked for many years as a factor in mental stability, so has exercise.

In our recent study of seven hundred doctors and their wives, we checked their daily exercise regimen, or lack of it, as well as their diets. Compared with those who led a sedentary life, those who exercised daily reported fewer physical problems and *half* as many psychological complaints. Using a computerized psychological score based on reported emotional symptoms, we found that the average score for exercisers was 1.6, while nonexercisers averaged 2.5, a 56 percent higher score.

Why? Because physical activity increases circulation through the body; exercising helps all the brain cells receive the nutrients they need. For many people, "nervous fatigue" is actually an indication of a sluggish circulation.

Exercisers tend to worry less, and with good reason. A two-year follow-up study of over a million men and women between the ages of forty-five and eighty-four demonstrated an inverse relationship between exercise and mortality. Among the men, a progressively lower death rate was observed as the amount of exercise increased. For men fifty to fifty-four, the deaths per hundred were: no exercise, 2.08; slight exercise, 0.80; moderate exercise, 0.55; strenuous exercise, 0.33. Between the extremes of "no exercise" and "strenuous exercise" there was more than a sixfold difference.

A research team from Purdue University has shown that rigorous physical conditioning can cause personality changes in middle-aged men. They tested a group before and after a four-month calisthenics and running program. At the start, those men in poor physical condition showed more signs of emotional distress on standard psychological test questionnaires then those who were in good condition. After the four-month program, virtually no difference in the emotional stability of any of the men could be discovered.

An exercise program brought unexpected results at the Alcoholic Rehabilitation Center at the Long Beach Naval Station. Three psychologists, who believed that their alcoholic patients continued to drink because of a poor self-image, initiated an exercise and jogging program to reduce their patients' weight and improve their physical condition. After several weeks, personality tests showed that while the alcoholics' health had greatly improved, they still held mighty low opinions of themselves.

Despite this, other benefits accrued as they continued to exercise. They slept better, were more active and alert, and chose more nutritious foods from the chow line. The hoped-for turnabout, a sharpened interest in attending therapy sessions and A.A. meetings, was triggered by the exercise program. The exercise, along with improved nutrition, proved to be the key to getting many of them off the bottle.

The benefits of exercise and good nutrition go hand in hand. In the study mentioned earlier, we found that the exercisers consumed approximately the same number of total calories as the nonexercisers, yet had a higher intake of every vitamin, mineral, and amino acid studied. They also consumed far less coffee, tea, alcohol, tobacco, sugar, and refined carbohydrates.

There are subtle reasons why the physically active are likely to prefer more nutritious foods than the sedentary. Exercising helps control blood-glucose levels and thus aids in preventing the hypoglycemic cycle, with its craving for sweets and stimulants. Controlled exercise programs have even helped diabetics get along with lower insulin doses.

Exercise can replace tranquilizers, and should, says Dr. Herbert de Vries, a researcher at the Ethel Percy Andrus Gerontology Center at the University of Southern California. He notes that tranquilizers, unlike exercise, frequently produce unpleasant side effects and slow reaction time. He has found that as little as fifteen minutes of exercise can alleviate short-term stress and even reduce long-term nervous tension.

Dr. de Vries monitored electrical activity in the muscles of a selected group of patients before and after exercising. The 20 percent drop registered after exercise remained in effect for more than one hour. Patients who continued regular exercise on a long-term basis demonstrated a 25 percent drop in nervous activity.

Richard Velde, deputy administrator of the Law Enforcement

Administration in Washington, D.C., feels he has developed "a whole new personality" since he started jogging regularly. He was so impressed by the psychological benefits he experienced that he has instituted exercise therapy for convicted felons, in the hope of improving their emotional adjustment before they are freed from jail.

If you have been exercising regularly and eating properly and you still are having trouble reaching a high degree of physical fitness, the missing element may be *octacosanol*, a substance found in wheat germ oil. After twenty years of research under controlled conditions with almost a thousand people—middle-aged university faculty members, fraternity men, schoolboys, swimmers, wrestlers, track men—there is abundant evidence that octacosanol has beneficial effects on exercisers. It improves their stamina and endurance, reduces heart stress, and quickens reaction time.

Do nutritionists have all the answers?

No. We're not even sure we know all the proper questions to ask, any more than do scientists in other fields. Environmentally created emotional disturbances emanate from a variety of sources: from the oft-discussed sociological and psychological assaults to the rarely discussed silent sounds to the sources of stress not yet identified.

We *do* know that good nutrition and daily exercise are important adjuncts to treatments for a variety of emotional disturbances, regardless of their origin. Viewed in this context, diet and exercise would seem to be your least expensive, most-easily-come-by defense against antagonistic forces.

11

Are You Going to Crack Up?

She was a fashionably dressed, rather fidgety woman who perched on the edge of a chair as though ready to jump up at any moment. A quick glance at her examination record showed that she was forty-two, married sixteen years, and had been recommended by a former patient.

"My friend Doris insisted I come here. She swears by your vitamin-diet treatments, but her case was simple compared to mine. I want to know where I stand before I go through the rigamarole of tests."

Mrs. L. paused for breath, then confessed that she lived in fear of suffering from an emotional breakdown someday.

"I've gone through so much. My father died when I was a baby, and my mother remarried an alcoholic who always took his drunken rages out on me. Since mom worked all the time to keep us kids fed, she was never around when I really needed her. I've always been nervous and insecure, but with such a childhood, what can you expect?"

We could see that Mrs. L. was voicing long-term concerns and that there would be more to her story. But before she continued, we had her fill out a brief questionnaire to help determine the possibility of an imminent emotional disorder. Try the questions she answered on yourself.

Have you *recently:*

1. been unable to concentrate on whatever you're doing?
2. lost much sleep from worrying?
3. felt that you are not playing a useful part in things?
4. felt that you are not able to make decisions about things?
5. felt constantly under strain?
6. felt that you couldn't overcome your difficulties?
7. been unable to enjoy your day-to-day activities?
8. been unable to face up to your problems?
9. been feeling unhappy and depressed?
10. been losing confidence in yourself?
11. been thinking of yourself as a worthless person?
12. found you cannot keep yourself busy and occupied?
13. been staying in the house more than usual?
14. been feeling on the whole that you were not doing things well?
15. been dissatisfied with the way you've carried out your tasks?
16. been taking things too hard?
17. found everything getting to be too much for you?
18. been feeling nervous and hung-up all the time?
19. found at times you couldn't do anything because your nerves were too bad?
20. been having restless, disturbed nights?
21. not been managing as well as most people in your place?
22. felt less warmth and affection for those near to you?
23. been finding it difficult to get along with other people?
24. spent much less time talking to people?
25. been finding life a struggle all the time?
26. been getting scared or panicky for no good reason?
27. felt that life is entirely hopeless?
28. been discouraged about your own future?
29. felt that life isn't worth living?

If, like Mrs. L., you answered yes to several of the 29 questions, you *may* have an emotional illness lurking just below the surface.

"Don't be alarmed," we told Mrs. L. "Your score isn't high, and even people who can honestly answer no to all those questions aren't necessarily immune from future emotional complaints."

Like many people, Mrs. L. believed her upbringing had marked her as a future psychiatric candidate. Among the many theories as to why emotional ailments develop is the rarely questioned belief that early parental influences are the prime factors in determining who will remain sane throughout life and who will crack under stress.

Standard textbooks speak in vague terms of the risk factors which make people prone to mental ailments: you are more likely to develop some mental malady if you come from a broken home, if one or both of your parents is or was an alcoholic, and so on.

Parent-child relationships have been subjected to an extraordinary amount of scrutiny in the search for predictive clues. The result is confusion. One hundred years ago, psychiatrists were convinced that much mental illness was the result of excessive parental discipline; today an equal number of experts are certain it is the result of too little.

Mrs. L. appeared somewhat relieved by our explanation, but she was still troubled.

"You haven't heard the worst—I've got two more strikes against me. My grandmother on my mother's side died in a mental institution, my uncle on my father's side had a nervous breakdown last summer, my sister is—well, peculiar. I've heard mental illness runs in families. Isn't it likely I'll crack up someday too?"

Many people are haunted by their ancestry, and, like Mrs. L., live in lifelong fear, wondering whether a mental breakdown lurks in ambush. We know of no psychiatric Jeane Dixon. Scientific expertise is noticeably imprecise when it comes to defining those predictive factors that lead to mental illness.

Authorities who find early childhood influences an unsatisfactory explanation often focus instead on heredity. Researchers dedicated to discovering genetic determinants for mental illness have enjoyed some success through studies on twins in compiling statistics which *appear* to indicate genetic influence as a primary factor.

Since children do look like their parents and often mimic their idiosyncrasies in a subtle way, it would be foolhardy to dismiss completely the possibility that genetic determinants are at work.

It is equally foolhardy, however, to place undue emphasis on genetics, since heredity and environment interact. The overlay of environment on heredity can often distort data which seemingly support the "inherited illness" theory.

Genetic theories are popular with the public; they offer people a convenient "out" for their problems. For example, overweight people frequently excuse themselves by saying, "I can't help being fat. My grandfather was fat, my mother is fat, my father is fat. It runs in our family."

Something other than heredity should be suspected when, as is frequently the case, the family dog is also fat! The fact that everyone under that roof habitually eats too much shouldn't be overlooked.

When we first began to suspect an overemphasis on genetics, many years ago, we undertook a health study of married couples which gave us a model for comparing the relative role of genetics and environment.

There's a familiar saying: "If you live with someone long enough, you get to look like them." That's often true, but why? Physical similarities between spouses, we reasoned, had to be based on environmental rather than genetic influences, it being quite unfashionable even nowadays for men to marry their sisters (or any blood relative).

One of our earliest discoveries was that men and women married for some time tend to develop similar health problems. Husbands who get headaches are frequently married to headachy women; men who are overweight are likely to have wives who need to lose weight; thin men generally have thin wives. There were very few Jack Sprat couples among the hundreds we have studied.

Married couples tend to become physiological twins as the wedding anniversaries accumulate: blood pressure, weight, drinking and smoking habits, general health, heart condition, even the chemical composition of their blood (cholesterol level and enzyme activity) very often match. Such similarities are likely to become most pronounced at or about the fifteenth year of marriage.

We were particularly intrigued by our discovery that the long-married become psychological twins as well. Men with many emotional problems live with women who report a correspondingly large number, usually of a similar type; men with few emotional complaints are wedded to women whose list is equally short.

Delving further, we found this to be no simple case of "like seeking like." The common supposition that men with mental problems invariably seek out their emotionally unstable counterparts happens to be untrue. Our evidence shows that emotional patterns between men and women are *not* similar during the early years of marriage, but tend to become more and more so with the passage of time.

Since we knew our married couples did not share ancestry, were subjected to vastly different childhood traumas, yet became more and more alike over the years, we searched their life styles for determining factors. Those who had been married fifteen years or longer have slept some 4,000 nights or more in the same room, eaten perhaps 56,000 meals together, and may have shared an equal number of between-meal snacks.

Could we find significant differences between the foods regularly eaten by those couples with few emotional problems and those with many? We set out to uncover both the "resistance" factors and the "susceptibility" factors in the diets of those who shrugged off stress and in the diets of those who were more vulnerable to stress. Resistance factors discourage disease (vitamin C, for example, discourages scurvy and is a resistance factor); susceptibility factors invite disease (sugar, which encourages dental cavities, is a susceptibility factor).

None of our testing subjects was suffering from a classic psychiatric disorder, but all six hundred of them were interested in

assessing their future mental health. Long before a mental breakdown takes place, there is a period of time during which minor
emotional problems appear. If the underlying causes are not found
and corrected, difficulties accumulate and intensify.

Each subject in our study received an annual examination, including an electrocardiogram, biochemical tests, and a detailed
dietary analysis. Each participant also filled out questionnaires
designed to evaluate his or her psychological status. The quizzes
(the Cornell Medical Index Health Questionnaire and the Cornell
Word Form-2) provided us with detailed information on each
subject's attitudes, moods and feelings, emotional and physical
reactions.

At every visit, each subject gave us a complete record of everything eaten during the previous seven-day period and filled out a
food-frequency questionnaire that revealed their eating patterns
and habits.

We submitted all of the data to computer analysis, and received
in return specific information concerning each subject's daily intake of various foods, plus the amounts of vitamins, minerals,
amino acids, and other known essential nutrients. By analyzing the
data, we established relationships between eating habits and mental health. From these relationships, we were able to determine the
likelihood of future emotional problems developing.

We divided the subject population into two groups: Group A
subjects were those with *no* emotional complaints; Group B subjects reported *one* or more. On the surface these two groups were
not particularly dissimilar; nutritionally, there were significant
differences. Group A's consumed distinctly higher amount of
most essential brain-cell nutrients: 12 percent more iron, 21
percent more iodine, 14 percent more niacin, and so on down the
list.

A complete processing of the data identified the many nutrients
that were possibly keeping the zero-complaint Group A's in better
shape than the Group B's. In addition to the three nutrients already

mentioned, we found phosphorous, thiamin, riboflavin, animal protein, vitamin C, vitamin A, and vegetable protein—additional resistance factors that helped the emotionally stable Group A's ward off difficulties.

When this information was cross-referenced as a check on our findings (substituting data from the "eating habits" questionnaire for data from the "seven-day dietary report"), additional nutrients showed up as more prominent in the Group A's diet: pantothenic acid, pyridoxine, vitamin B_{12}, tryptophane, vitamin E, methionine, leucine, threonine, phenylalanine, and potassium—more resistance factors.

Looking at the data from yet another angle, we found that Group A's not only ate more of these resistance nutrients, they also ate far *less* of other types of foods: white-flour products, sugar and sugar-filled items—the refined carbohydrate substances which were obviously susceptibility factors, since the subjects who ate the most of them also had the most emotional complaints.

Despite different backgrounds and life experiences, our subjects' *current* emotional balance seemed to be directly influenced by what they ate. When we reported our findings to the test subjects, the group B's were understandably eager to improve their status. Many of them decided to change their eating habits and see what would happen.

Thirty-one increased their intake of tryptophane, the essential amino acid found in animal protein, eggs, milk, and milk products. Tested again a year later, they averaged a 50 percent decrease in emotional complaints. A few subjects tried adding a vitamin-mineral supplement to their diet for one full year. When retested, they too showed a noticeable decrease in emotional complaints.

In each instance, the change in diet made the subject less prone to future emotional problems, as well as relieving the symptoms they were already reporting.

We summarized all these findings for Mrs. L., who listened closely.

"Then all I really have to do to stay sane," she said, "is swallow a few vitamin pills and change my diet. Right?"

Wrong. *No* therapy can make such a promise. We do know this: the more resistance factors and the fewer susceptibility factors you get from your diet, the better prepared you will be to weather whatever emotional storms await you.

Anyone concerned about his future mental health should think about his diet. Keep a seven-day diary of everything you eat and drink. Then examine the list carefully.

Lots of refined carbohydrates? Sugar? White-flour foods? Desserts? Starchy sweets? Eat-and-run packaged foods? Sweetened drinks?

You're placing yourself in danger.

Does your diet largely consist of meat, eggs, poultry, fish, whole-grain cereals, fresh fruits, nuts, seeds, dairy products, fresh vegetables?

Then you're fortifying yourself against future problems.

If you take a balanced vitamin-mineral supplement (see Chapter 13) that contains all of the essential and nonessential elements, you've increased your chances of becoming a zero-complaint person.

It all adds up to an understanding that no one need feel helpless about preventing a mental crackup. Your chance of remaining emotionally stable is likely to depend more upon your internal environment—the way you eat—than on any of the external forces which may come along.

Dr. Jacques M. May put it very well indeed: "It is as though I had on a table three dolls, one made of glass, another of celluloid, and a third of steel, and I chose to hit the three dolls with a hammer using equal strength. The first doll would break, the second would scar, the third would emit a pleasant sound."

You can decide which kind of doll you want to be: the one that shatters under assault, the one that survives but is scarred for life, or the one that remains resilient through adversity.

Will Mrs. L. crack up?

She has taken important steps to lessen the likelihood. We arranged for a complete set of biochemical tests, did an analysis of her eating habits, and then prescribed a regimen in which resistance factors far outweighed susceptibility factors in her diet.

The many people who share Mrs. L.'s fear should take heart, keeping in mind that people exposed to the same "psychic germs" react quite differently. Evaluate your own eating habits, or have a computerized analysis done for you (see Appendix B).

Are you going to crack up?

It's up to you.

12

The Balanced-Diet Myth

Social commentators who have dubbed recent decades "The Age of Anxiety" normally recite a long list of increasing social pressures as the basic cause of America's number-one health problem: mental illness.

Emotional ailments, *which now hospitalize as many victims as all other illnesses combined,* have escalated sharply in recent years. On any given day, there are some 753,000 people under psychiatric care in hospitals alone, plus an additional 173,000 being treated through some form of supervised community care. Add to this the 1,350,000 outpatients served by private and public clinics, and we find three and one-half to four million Americans receiving some form of psychotherapy, or one in fifty. According to the United States Bureau of the Census, that is over twice the number treated for mental illness in 1944.

Omitted from these figures are most of the nine million clearly recognized alcoholics, an unreported population of drug addicts, and those who suffer less specific mental ailments, from excess fatigue to psychosomatic complaints, without getting caught up in the statistics.

The increase in such problems among young people is particularly alarming. Ten per cent of all school-age children have emotional difficulties requiring psychiatric treatment, and *more than a million children* now have such serious mental disorders as schizophrenia or other psychotic illnesses.

Dr. Joseph Noshpitz, president of the American Academy of Child Psychiatry, claims that if really careful screening devices were used, statistics would probably be doubled or trebled.

As public costs for mental illness have doubled in recent years (from $20 billion in 1966, according to the *Medical Tribune,* to an estimated $40 billion today), investigators have searched every aspect of daily life to explain the nation's deteriorating mental stability; every aspect, that is, but the nation's eating habits. Very few have made a connection between the climbing rate of mental illness and the progressive worsening of the American diet.

In the most recent national study of what families eat, released by the Department of Agriculture, we find that of the 7500 households surveyed, *only half* had diets that met Recommended Dietary Allowances for calories, protein, calcium, iron, vitamin A, thiamine, riboflavin, and ascorbic acid. The other half had diets that failed to meet the allowances for one or more of these essentials. The diets of one in five families were rated *poor!*

The percentage of *good* diets dropped from 60 percent of all households in 1955 to 50 percent in 1965, while diets rated *poor* increased from 15 percent to 20 percent. Calcium, vitamin A, and ascorbic acid were the nutrients most often found to be in short supply.

The devastating decline in nutritional quality can be partially explained by a grocery dollar shift toward foods offering little but calories. Americans are buying less milk and dairy products but more soft drinks, punches, ades, and alcoholic beverages; less fresh citrus fruit but more frozen juices and lemonade; less fresh and more processed potatoes; more canned, frozen, precooked, ready-to-serve items in place of prepared-at-home foods; more potato chips, crackers, cookies, doughnuts, ice cream, and candy, all eat-and-run items filled with sugar, starch, and chemical additives.

The survey compared age groups. Nutritionally, elderly persons fared the worst. Adolescents from ten to sixteen years of age ate almost as poorly. Low income helps explain the diet deficiencies found among senior citizens. Among the young, poor food choices are likely to be the villain.

One of the shockers of the study was that high income does *not* insure good nutrition. An analysis of diet and income revealed that 37 percent of the households with upper-middle-class incomes had diets deficient in one or more essential nutrients.

A 1972 study we made confirms the extent to which choice rather than low budget accounts for poor diet. We asked 364 doctors and 296 of their wives, in five sections of the country, to keep detailed records of what they ate and drank. Upon calculating the results, we found that 12 percent of the doctors consumed less than the Recommended Daily Allowance for vitamin B_3; 10 percent did not get enough vitamin C; 32 percent did not get enough calcium; approximately half were not getting enough vitamin E; and 95 percent were not getting minimum recommended amounts of iodine.

The doctors' wives were doing even worse, and both groups were found to rely far too heavily on refined carbohydrates.

Considering the way they eat, it is not surprising that most doctors remain relatively unknowledgeable about the relationship between diet and mental health. Rarely do they ask their "tense" patients, "What do you eat?"

Governmental guardians who constantly assure us we are the world's healthiest people attempt to perpetuate the myth that "three square meals a day" will provide anyone all the nourishment needed. Dr. C. E. Butterworth, chairman of the Council on Foods and Nutrition of the American Medical Association, recently stated: "All the recommended nutrient intakes considered essential to the maintenance of health in normal individuals can be provided by a balanced diet of conventional foods including enriched and fortified items."

This "balanced diet" myth conveniently ignores these facts:

American food habits are indeed moving from bad to worse.

Soil and growth conditions vary drastically from one part of the country to another, making it virtually impossible to assess the nutrient values of foods produced.

Refinement and processing rob food of vital substances.

Little professional agreement exists as to what a "balanced diet" is or for whom it is "balanced."

Dr. Carlton Fredericks is one well-known nutrition expert who believes the "balanced diet" to be nonexistent. Testifying at the October 1973 congressional hearings before the House Subcommittee on Public Health and Environment, he mentioned that a group of experts, assembled by NASA to lay down the guidelines for supplying optimal nutrition to astronauts on a five-month flight, had disbanded after only twenty-four hours of discussion because they could not arrive at a consensus on the first item on the agenda, calories.

Dr. Fredericks pointed out that these scientists had been handed an impossible task. The science of nutrition is still largely in its infancy, and individual requirements for carbohydrates, fats, protein, vitamins, and minerals have yet to be standardized in any textbook. Confronted with a decision involving optimal intake as opposed to minimal maintenance, it's hardly surprising that the "experts" exploded with frustration.

Even assuming that a balanced diet had been scientifically established, which it has not, what would the odds be of choosing foods to fit the formula? A thousand-to-one shot, at best; a poor gamble, considering the stakes. Today's edibles, grown on mineral-depleted soils, manufactured with an eye to appearance, and processed to last on store shelves, have lost nutritional value every step of the way.

As a result of technological manipulation, items formerly considered "highly nutritious" are hardly worth being called "foods" any longer. A clever chemical feast masquerades as yesterday's ice cream. Those who think they are enjoying a wholesome dairy product might find their enjoyment dimmed if the package alerted them to the fact that most frozen desserts contain antioxidants, neutralizers, buffers, bactericides, surfactants, stabilizers, and emulsifiers.

Except for those brands whose packages properly proclaim them to be "natural," ice cream is likely to offer you alcohol, propylene glycol, vanillin, methyl salicylate, and ethyl acetate, substances as bad for you as they are hard to pronounce. Ethyl acetate, for example, is primarily a textile and leather cleaner. Its vapors have been known to cause lung, liver, and heart damage.

Food "faddists" who once held center stage in complaints about processed and devitaminized foods have been vindicated. All recent tests confirm that foods lose important nutrients as they travel from the garden to the stomach. Those made from refined grains fare the worst. Bread, once the "staff of life," hardly resembles its former self. Wheat transformed into white flour loses more than 50 percent of its health-giving vitamins and almost 90 percent of its minerals.

One of the great nutritional travesties is that many products made from virtually valueless flour are now labeled "enriched." Over twenty nutrients are taken out, four are put back! Yet the public is constantly propagandized into believing they are buying a superior product.

Dr. Joe Nichols graphically describes this "enrichment" process:

Suppose a mugger ordered you at gun point to strip down to your birthday suit, giving up clothing, shoes, underwear, wallet, credit cards, jewelry—everything you possess. Then, should the thief take pity on you and return your wedding band, your socks, and perhaps your topcoat to cover your nakedness so you could get home, you might feel "enriched," but I doubt it. That's the equivalent of what's taking place in the food industry. First they strip away everything of value—then they put back a token selection of necessities and convince everyone they've been "enriched" by the process.

In one research project, two-thirds of the rats kept on a ninety-day diet of bread made from "enriched" wheat flour *died*. This is a dramatic illustration of the life-threatening aspects of nutritional depletion.

Foods continue to run a nutritional obstacle course when they reach the kitchen. Heat is the greatest single food-value wrecker. Many items, which have already been mortally wounded by being blanched, sterilized, dehydrated, pasteurized, toasted, smoked, puffed, or roasted, are then cooked to death at home. Canned peas, for example, have lost 94 percent of their original value by the time they are eaten. The frozen variety lose 59 percent by the time they are thawed, 83 percent by the time they are cooked and eaten. Even *fresh* peas lose 56 percent of their original vitamins during preparation.

Homemakers who brag about stretching leftovers shouldn't. Twice-heated foods are less than half as good as they were the first time around; pennies saved, dollars wasted on future visits to the doctor.

"Eating out" presents the ultimate hazard. Restaurants that keep foods hot on steam tables and simmer stoves might just as well serve their customers the cooking utensils for all the nutrition they're dishing out. Fast-food, quick-serve dining spots keep frankfurters and hamburgers warm for hours and are indeed able to speed customers down the road—to physical and mental health problems.

Even when we're "eating in" we're "eating out," for most homemakers make heavy use of "instant" precooked foods. Television commercials reinforce this trend, often suggesting that a modern female who does anything more than add boiling water to a "ready mix" is retreating into medieval drudgery.

How *do* most Americans eat? By all reports, badly and inconsistently. Meal skipping is on the rise, with 8 to 14 percent of most age groups bypassing lunch (in the late teens and early twenties, 20 percent). Every fourth person skips breakfast, the most important meal of the day. The coffee-and-a-doughnut replacement is on the rise for all ages, at all income levels.

Are you getting the fifty or more essential nutrients required for emotional health?

Are your eating habits promoting mental stability by increasing your body's resistance to stress?

To find out, answer yes or no to the following questions:

1. Are you on a special diet (to lose weight, low salt, diabetic, low cholesterol, or because of food allergy)?   yes   no
2. Is your appetite frequently poor?   yes   no
3. Do you usually skip one or more meals a day?   yes   no
4. Do you frequently consume sweet foods or drinks between meals?   yes   no
5. Do you often feel shaky or weak if you do not eat on time?   yes   no
6. Do you usually drink some form of alcoholic beverage (whiskey, beer, wine) daily?   yes   no
7. Do you usually drink coffee or tea more than three times each day?   yes   no
8. Do you usually use sugar in your coffee or tea?   yes   no
9. Do you usually eat desserts once or more each day?   yes   no
10. Do you frequently use low calorie (dietetic, artificially sweetened) foods and drink or artificial sweeteners (like saccharin)?   yes   no
11. Do you consume soft drinks of the regular kind almost daily?   yes   no
12. Do you eat starch foods frequently (macaroni, bread, biscuits, breakfast cereals, cornbread)?   yes   no
13. Do you frequently eat sweets (sugar, syrup, jams, jellies, candy)?   yes   no
14. Do you frequently eat bakery products (cakes, pies, cookies, doughnuts, pancakes)?   yes   no
15. Do you frequently eat ice cream, ice milk, or canned or frozen fruits?   yes   no

16. Do you usually add salt to your foods at the table? yes no
17. Do you usually eat meat (such as beef, chicken, pork) less than twice a day? yes no
18. Do you often omit eggs? yes no
19. Do you omit seafoods from your diet? yes no
20. Do you usually avoid milk, cheese, butter? yes no
21. Do you avoid raw vegetables (lettuce, tomatoes, carrots, etc.)? yes no
22. Do you eat green or yellow vegetables less than twice daily? yes no
23. Do you usually avoid citrus fruits or juices? yes no
24. Do you usually avoid other types of fresh raw fruits or juices? yes no
25. Do you usually omit vitamin or mineral supplements daily? yes no

Add up the yes answers and multiply by four. Your score will lie somewhere between 0 and 100. The closer to 0 you score, the better your diet. On the other hand, as your score climbs, your proneness to mental illness increases.

As you work toward changing your eating habits until they conform to the Optimal Diet, check your progress from time to time with this test. As your score improves, you will find yourself in a happier frame of mind.

Is the balanced diet a myth? Obviously.

Set your sights on the Optimal Diet instead, and reap the rewards.

13

The Optimal Diet

Kitty is assembling her family's food supplies for the week. As she makes her way up and down the supermarket aisles she's outwardly serene, inwardly in turmoil.

"Eggs? No, they raise cholesterol levels. Chocolate cookies? The kids will howl if I don't buy them. How bad can they be? Potatoes are on sale. Better not, they're starchy. Margarine or butter? Wish I could remember what I read about that. Bananas should be safe. Did someone tell me they're gassed before picking? Oh, my God, I wish I knew what I was doing."

Do you approach your food shopping with similar confusion? Have all the nutritionists' warnings left you feeling totally inadequate in the supermarket?

Dr. Michael Jacobson, a food scientist with the Center for Science in the Public Interest, believes the average shopper has a lot to learn. In his view the country's major food marketers are cunning adversaries, dedicated to "private wealth" rather than "public health," and he advises consumers to grow adept at identifying their devious ways. The following quiz, designed to assess your nutritional know-how, was prepared with his help. Select the answer, (A) or (B), you think most appropriate:

1. A number of food additives have been linked to detrimental health effects. If you were trying to avoid the two *worst* additives,

you would read labels carefully to steer away from products containing (A) Polysorbate-60 and EDTA; (B) sugar and artificial coloring.

2. Fiber or roughage is removed from wheat and rice when they are processed. Since fiber does not contain any vitamins or minerals, it is nutritionally worthless. (A) True; (B) False.

3. You are sure to increase the nutritional adequacy of your diet by carefully choosing foods labeled as having been "enriched" during manufacture. (A) True; (B) False.

4. All fruits are good and nutritious, but the one that contains the most vitamins per average serving is (A) a wedge of watermelon; (B) an apple.

5. A wise choice for a nutritious and healthy dessert is fruit-flavored gelatin. (A) True; (B) False.

6. The riboflavin (vitamin B_2) that is contained in milk is best protected against loss by (A) a waxed-paper carton; (B) a clear glass bottle.

7. Meat is an excellent source of protein. You are making a better nutritional buy when purchasing (A) choice or prime cuts of beef; (B) good or standard grades of beef.

8. If you were relying on carrots for your daily vitamin A supply, you would be wise to eat (A) raw young tender carrots; (B) steamed or boiled older mature carrots.

Think you did pretty well? Score yourself as follows:

Question 1.	(A) 1 point;	(B) 2 points
Question 2.	(A) 1 point;	(B) 2 points
Question 3.	(A) 1 point;	(B) 2 points
Question 4.	(A) 2 points;	(B) 1 point
Question 5.	(A) 1 point;	(B) 2 points
Question 6.	(A) 2 points;	(B) 1 point
Question 7.	(A) 1 point;	(B) 2 points
Question 8.	(A) 1 point;	(B) 2 points

Only those who score a perfect 16 points have the nutritional sophistication to saunter down the supermarket aisles and emerge unscathed.

Dr. Jacobson booby-trapped the quiz with a couple of sneaky questions. For example, carrots do not contain much vitamin A until they mature, and what vitamin A they do contain is locked into a strong cellulose structure. That makes carrots one of the few vegetables providing more nutrition cooked than raw.

A perfect score, however, is no guarantee that you will not fall victim to some of the newer advertising gimmicks. Food manufacturers, well aware of growing public interest in nutrition, are pushing worthless fad foods as "fortified." In reality, they offer no better nutrition than a starchy, low-quality vitamin pill.

It takes a special kind of expertise to know there is more nourishment in Alpo Dog Food than in a drive-in's hamburger. According to Dr. Jacobson, Alpo also rates higher than pork chops, shrimp, boiled or sliced ham, higher, even, than sirloin steak. Until nutritional labeling on foods meant for humans provides information as accurate as that found on most products packaged for pets, a conscientious shopper is distinctly at a disadvantage.

Supermarket shelves are packed full of incredible edibles, more toys than real foods. *Quik, ee-zee* or *redi*, they have a nutritional content as atrocious as their spelling.

One cardinal rule sums up what you need to know: *Avoid as much as possible those foods that have been refined or processed and that contain food additives and chemical pollutants.* The less doctored foods you choose, the less likely you'll need doctoring yourself.

The prettier the package, the more suspect is the food. Those colorful boxes may even be more nutritious than the contents. A biochemist at the University of Georgia chose one of the new, attractive-to-the-kiddies-cereals, emulsified both the box and the cereal, then fed one white rat the box and another the cereal. The one that ate the box thrived better.

Develop a reading-habit—label reading—when it comes to selecting cereals as well as other foods. Cereals which have been puffed, popped, sugared, and colored are to be avoided, for they contain chemicals designed to increase their shelf life, not yours.

The average adult yearly intake of food additives, in addition to 115 pounds of sugar and 15 pounds of salt, includes 8.4 pounds of corn syrup, 4.2 pounds of dextrose (glucose), and 10 pounds of about 2000 other additives. You can significantly reduce your chemical consumption by taking the time to read food labels each time you shop.

At first you will be discouraged. You'll find yourself rejecting an enormous number of items you previously popped automatically into the market basket. But if you persist, your disposition and finances will both improve. Whatever television commercials tell you, junk and convenience foods are the most expensive. Try not to be influenced by advertising. Those foods with the least nutritional value are often the subjects of Madison Avenue's cleverest, most expensive campaigns. When was the last time you saw a TV ad for fresh fruits or vegetables?

Your best Cook's Tour through a landmined food market is our Optimal Diet. Based on the findings explained in Chapter 11, it clearly distinguishes good foods from bad and emphasizes the need for essential nutrients. The Optimal Diet is, in one sense, *not* a "diet." There are no menus for you to follow, no calories or carbohydrates to count, you need not measure or weigh portions of food. All foods are categorized into three easy-to-remember groups: *Foods to Eat Liberally, Foods to Eat Sparingly,* and *Foods to Avoid.* You can develop rational eating habits for the rest of your life by choosing foods according to the Optimal Diet guidelines.

How liberally? How sparingly? Portions should be adjusted to suit appetite and individual goals. Both the underweight and the overweight, as well as those with special nutritional needs, find that the Optimal Diet gradually readjusts their metabolic balance, thereby eliminating food-related problems.

- **Foods to Eat Liberally**

Foods containing nutrients that enhance the body's defenses against disease should be your mainstay. These *resistance nutrients*, which include protein, vitamins, minerals, and essential fats, are found in a variety of wholesome foods.

The most nutritious protein foods, those containing all the essential amino acids in proper balance, are obtained largely from animal sources: meat, fish, fowl, eggs, cheese, and milk. Since these foods can effectively replace daily body protein losses, they are said to have a high "biologic value." Whole-egg protein has a biologic value of 100 percent, meaning it replaces, gram for gram, daily protein losses. The relative value of other proteins are: animal protein (meat, fish, fowl), 70–100 percent; milk protein (milk, cheese), 70–75 percent; vegetable protein (fruit, vegetables, grains) 40–65 percent.

Many of the foods we are recommending you eat "liberally" —eggs, dairy products, fish, and meat—may be the very items you have been avoiding, for fear their cholesterol content will raise your blood cholesterol levels. Eggs, for example, have been foolishly villified as a killer food, thanks to the simplistic and incorrect notion that the cholesterol in your blood comes directly from the cholesterol you eat. Most of it does not.

Eighty percent of the cholesterol in your blood is manufactured within the body by the liver and other organs. It is synthesized from acetate radicals found in carbohydrates, proteins, and fats into cholesterol. Only 20 percent of the cholesterol in your blood comes directly from preformed dietary cholesterol. The amount of cholesterol in the diet is not a significant factor in the development of atherosclerosis for the vast majority of people, since the human liver ordinarily synthesizes far more cholesterol than is obtained from foods.

There is general misunderstanding of the cholesterol problem because high serum cholesterol is the result of internal metabolism. Some of the cholesterol problem comes from an unsuspected source—refined carbohydrates which furnish large amounts of acetate radicals. Some of the cholesterol problem is related to a lack of nutrients. Lecithin, vitamin C, nicotinic acid, and grain and vegetable fiber are all cholesterol lowering agents and help the body to regulate cholesterol levels. Eggs are particularly rich in lecithin, the very substance medical researchers have shown to be cholesterol-controlling.

Eliminating foods containing cholesterol from your diet can actually escalate a cholesterol problem since there is ample evidence that when a diet is deficient in pre-formed cholesterol, a complicated feedback system goes into operation which encourages the body to manufacture excess amounts of this substance.

If your doctor has placed you on a low cholesterol diet, discuss these matters with him before adopting the Optimal Diet.

Eggs. Eat at least one egg each day; eat two if you enjoy them. The eggs will furnish more nutrients per calorie than any other single food except milk.

Scavenging the supermarket for egg substitute products is apt to prove a fruitless exercise. There is a four-to-one probability that you cannot eliminate your cholesterol problem by putting all your eggs in a nonegg basket.

Cheese. Use cheese freely in your diet for snacks or as a meat or milk substitute. Eat both hard cheese and cottage cheese in its natural state. In other words, eat whole, unprocessed cheese in preference to the types that you scoop out of jars, squeeze out of tubes, or spray out of cans. The latter are actually mixtures of cheese and other less nourishing foods and are chemically contaminated besides.

Milk. Milk can be consumed with meals or as a snack. Skimmed or low-fat milk, whether fresh or powdered, is preferable to whole milk if overweight is a problem. Generally, two glasses a day are sufficient. Fermented or cultured milk products such as yogurt and buttermilk have several advantages over sweet milk. The cultured product aids in the digestion and absorption of essential nutrients, by counteracting the discomfort suffered by those older people who lack the enzyme lactase and therefore cannot digest sweet milk. In addition, the microorganisms that ferment milk into buttermilk and yogurt continue their activity in the intestinal tract and actually contribute to the body's manufacture of essential vitamins.

Meat, Seafood, and Poultry. These foods should be eaten at least once each day; twice if you do not eat eggs. Give preference to the lean varieties of meat. Liver and other organ meats such as pancreas, kidney, tripe, and brain are also excellent high protein foods. Restrict fried meats. Before cooking beef, pork, and lamb servings, trim off as much fat as possible.

Since it takes five to six hours to digest meat, its consumption at the evening meal may cause indigestion and lead to a variety of other complaints, including allergies, skin disorders, arthritis, even mental illness. Eating meat at breakfast or lunch rather than dinner insures *complete* digestion and is one way of avoiding such problems.

Fruit and Fruit Juice. When available, fresh fruit should be eaten twice daily, with meals or as a snack. Ideally, one serving should be of a citrus variety. Raw fruit is preferable to cooked. If canned fruit, frozen fruit, or refrigerated bottled fruit is used, select unsweetened varieties packed in their natural juices or in water. Hypoglycemics and the overweight should avoid prunes, dates, raisins, and other dried fruits; those people who are underweight can benefit from their natural sugars.

Fruit juices may replace one serving of fresh fruit. If citrus juice is chosen, the fresh-fruit serving should not be citrus. Juices serve as substitutes for undesirable beverages such as coffee, tea, soft and alcoholic drinks. Any kind of fruit juice, canned, frozen, or fresh, is acceptable if no sugar has been added. If you are hypoglycemic or overweight, avoid grape or prune juice; the reverse applies to the underweight. Those who are overweight may prefer grapefruit to orange juice, since it has less natural sugar.

Vegetables. The list of nutrient-rich vegetables is almost endless; yet vegetables make up one of the two food groups most commonly absent from the average diet (the other is fruits). The Department of Agriculture reports that Americans consume 13 percent less fresh fruit and 7 percent less fresh vegetables than they did ten years ago. This decrease reflects the extent of current nutritional illiteracy.

Eat four or more servings of vegetables each day. When fresh varieties are not available or acceptable, use frozen or canned vegetables. Potatoes are satisfactory once a day. Whole potatoes, baked or boiled *with the skin intact*, provide the maximum nutritional value.

One vegetable serving each day should be a raw vegetable or vegetable salad. Tomatoes should be included frequently in this category, since they are an excellent source of Vitamins A and C. When the only tomatoes on the market have the winter blahs, raw green peppers can be added to your salads to supply the Vitamin C, and broccoli is one of the richest vegetable sources of both A and C.

Other vegetable servings should include—but need not be limited to—the dark-green or yellow varieties, for they are particularly rich in many valuable nutrients, such as iron, riboflavin and calcium. Almost every vegetable, from asparagus to zucchini, has something worthwhile to contribute to your well-being, but the types specified should be given preference because of their higher nutrient content. When vegetables are to be cooked, cook until just tender in as little water as possible to assure the best retention of vitamins and minerals.

Vegetable juice, with no sugar added, may replace one of the cooked vegetables or may serve as a mealtime beverage or as a snack.

Breads and Cereals. Try to eat four servings daily of *whole*-grain foods. Make your selection from: whole-grain breakfast cereals, wheat germ, 100-percent whole-wheat bread and flour, brown rice, and whole-grain corn meal. (Hypoglycemics need to restrict many of these foods. The overweight should eat skimpier portions—they should *not* be eliminated from the diet. The underweight should eat them freely.) Whole-grain cereals that require cooking, such as oatmeal and whole-wheat cereals, are the most nutritious.

If you prefer a precooked cereal, use the natural whole-grain varieties that do not contain chemical additives. Since these and all other precooked cereals contain sugar or honey, don't limit your breakfast to a bowl of cereal. It's a good idea to enrich the precooked cereal with one or two tablespoons each of toasted wheat germ, wheat bran and lecithin granules.

You can make a tasty "granola" that contains no sugar. Toast oatmeal flakes (three-minute oats) in the oven, and then add nuts, sunflower seeds, toasted wheat germ, wheat bran, and lecithin granules. Between your local health food store and your supermarket, you can find all these ingredients.

Buy 100 percent whole-wheat bread that contains no sugar or additives if you can get it. Even though the supermarket brands of 100 per cent whole wheat bread contain some sugar or molasses and additives, they are a good second choice.

Nuts and Seeds. These are valuable additions to your diet, and occasionally may be substituted for meat. They also supply essential fatty acids. Any of the dry-roasted nuts, as well as raw sunflower seeds, raw pumpkin seeds, or *nonhydrogenated* peanut butter, make nutritious between-meal snacks. If you have a blender, some roasted peanuts, and vegetable oil, you can make peanut butter quite easily in your own kitchen. The underweight may nibble freely on peanuts, almonds, pecans, walnuts, pistachio nuts, and cashews, but should avoid the varieties to which salt has been added.

• **Foods to Eat Sparingly**

The interpretation of "sparingly" depends upon a number of individual factors such as overweight, underweight, physical activity, cholesterol level, and hypoglycemia. The overweight, sedentary, or hypoglycemic person, for example, may need to reduce the daily servings of some "liberal" foods—fruit, fruit juice, bread, cereal, rice, potatoes, and corn. (The hypoglycemic diet in Appendix C shows you how to do this.) The underweight person may interpret "sparingly" much more "liberally."

Fat. Careful attention should be given to fat intake. When it comes to fats used as "spreads" on bread, potatoes, and for seasoning foods, a limited amount of butter is preferable to products made from hydrogenated (saturated) refined vegetable oil. An acceptable alternative is the recently introduced squeeze-bottle spread which has a much lower degree of hydrogenation.

Hydrogenated fats encourage a cholesterol problem, since they disturb cholesterol metabolism. The great bulk of fats in your diet will come from their use in cooking, salads, and mayonnaise, and you should be careful to select those fats from unrefined vegetable oils such as corn oil, peanut oil, cottonseed oil, or safflower seed oil. Of these, corn oil and safflower seed oil are the better choices, since they contain the largest amount of unsaturated fatty acids.

All of these oils, however, increase your need for vitamin E, and you should be sure you are getting more than a token amount of this essential nutrient.

Salt. Everyone would benefit from a *reduction* in salt intake; it is mandatory for those with high blood pressure or a tendency to retain fluid in their bodies.

Coffee and Tea. The nutritional value is negligible, so consume them sparingly and only with meals. Do not sweeten them with sugar. An artificial sweetener can be used frugally for these beverages (if you'll be miserable otherwise), but try to avoid using them to sweeten other foods.

Contrary to what many believe, there is no such thing as a "healthy" sugar. Brown sugar, raw sugar, turbinado, confectioner's sugar, and all such products are little better from a nutritional point of view than white table sugar, although some of them are extravagantly priced. They are all essentially the same—sucrose.

Substituting honey for table sugar can also present problems, but does hold certain advantages. Since honey is twice as sweet as sugar, you are likely to use smaller quantities. Also, the principal sweetening sugar in honey is fructose, which does not need as much insulin to be metabolized as the sucrose found in other sugars and is therefore preferable.

• Foods to Avoid

Obviously, foods that increase the likelihood of disease should be avoided: sugar, white flour, hydrogenated fat, food preservatives such as the nitrates and nitrites, and the many artificial flavoring and coloring agents.

While it may be virtually impossible to eliminate *all* these undesirable substances from your diet (it can be frustrating even to try), it is possible to cut intake as much as 75 percent by substituting foods from the "liberal" category.

Of all the foods to be avoided, sugar is the most harmful. It is a prominent factor in the development of overweight conditions and diabetes, hypoglycemia, dental cavities and periodontal disease, kidney stones, urinary infection, cardiovascular disease, intestinal cancer, diverticulosis, indigestion, hormone disorders—and mental illness.

Since the calories in sugar-rich foods are "empty" calories, they contribute very little to the body's need for vitamins, minerals, essential fats, and protein. At the same time, considerable quantities of such vitamins and minerals as thiamine (B_1), riboflavin (B_2), niacin (B_3), pyridoxine (B_6), pantothenic acid, phosphorus, and magnesium are necessary to metabolize sugar properly; thus, people who ingest sugar and sugary food instead of those rich in vitamins and minerals are bound to end up with vitamin deficiencies.

Sugar. Much harmful sugar is consumed unknowingly. Check labels carefully on the products you buy. Select unsweetened varieties when you have a choice. Refrain from using table sugar and from adding it to home-cooked foods. Popular foods with substantial sugar content include:

Food	Serving	Tsps. of Sugar
candy	chocolate bar, 1 average size	7
	chocolate fudge, 1½ in. sq.	4
	chocolate mints, 1 medium (20 to 1 lb.)	3
	chocolate cream, 1 average	2
	marshmallow, 1 large	1½
	chewing gum, 1 stick	½
cakes,	chocolate, 1/12 cake (2-layer iced)	15
cookies,	angel food, 1/12 of large cake	6
etc.	sponge, 1/10 of average cake	6
	cream puff, 1 custard-filled, iced	5
	doughnut, 3 in. diameter, plain	4
	macaroons, 1 large or 2 small	3
	brownies, 2 x 2 x ¾ in.	3
	molasses cookies, 3½ in. diameter	2
	gingersnaps, 1 medium	1
ice	sherbet, ½ cup	6–8
cream	ice cream, ½ cup	5–6
pie	cherry, 1/6 med. pie	14
	raisin, 1/6 med. pie	13
	apple, 1/6 med. pie	12
	pumpkin, 1/6 med. pie	10
soft	sweet flavored soda, 6 oz.	4⅓
drinks	ginger ale, 6 oz.	3⅓
milk	chocolate, 1 cup, 5 oz. milk	6
	eggnog, 1 glass, 8 oz. milk	4½
	cocoa, 1 cup, 5 oz. milk	4
spreads	chocolate sauce, 1 tbs. thick	4½
and	jam, 1 tbs. level	3
sauces	marmalade, 1 tbs. level	3
	jelly, 1 tbs. level	2½
	syrup, 1 tbs. level	2½

Food	Serving	Tsps. of Sugar
fruits	rhubarb, stewed, sweetened, ½ cup	8
	prunes, stewed, sweetened, 4 to 5 med., 2 tbs. juice	8
	fruit cocktail, ½ cup	5
	peaches, pears, canned in syrup, 2 halves, 1 tbs. syrup	3½

Omitted from this table prepared by the American Dental Association are the sweetened, precooked breakfast cereals, sweetened fruit juices, and sweetened breakfast drinks. Avoid them!

White Flour. Restrict your intake, as much as possible, of baked goods made from white flour: white bread, saltine and other crackers, rolls, buns, noodles, macaroni, spaghetti, and sweetened baked goods.

Don't let the label "enriched flour" fool you. Remember, of the twenty-odd different vitamins, minerals, and amino acids removed during the transformation of wheat into white flour, only *four* are put back. And even if all of them were replaced, there would still be an undetermined nutrient loss since all the essential substances have not as yet been identified. In one experiment, a biochemist took a natural bran product, carefully removed *all* of the known nutrients, then fed the supposedly worthless residue to a group of laboratory rats in addition to their regular diet. The rats thrived, compared to a control group not given the "worthless" supplement!

Hydrogenated Fat. Hydrogenated (hardened or saturated) vegetable oils such as oleomargarine, peanut butter containing hydrogenated oil, solid cooking fat made from vegetable oil, and coffee whiteners should be eliminated, as much as possible, from your diet.

Hydrogenated fat is the result of a chemical process by which liquid fats are hardened with hydrogen. This produces an unnaturally saturated fat which the body is not able to cope with successfully and disturbs cholesterol metabolism.

The only peanut butter, by the way, that does *not* contain hydrogenated oils will say so on the label. The new liquid margarines have a lower degree of hydrogenation and are therefore more unsaturated and preferable.

Most commercial baked goods, both sweetened and unsweetened, contain hydrogenated fat. Since they are usually made with sugar and white flour as well, you have a threefold reason for eliminating them from your diet.

Sodium Nitrate and Sodium Nitrite. These additives are used to cure, color, preserve, and flavor many meat products. They are frequently found in ham, bacon, sausage, canned and sliced luncheon meats, corned beef, salami, bologna, most frankfurters, liverwurst, and smoked fish.

Nitrates and nitrites can combine with other chemicals in your body or in these meats to form nitrosamines, which, in very small amounts, can contribute to cancer. They also cause indigestion, which can in turn lead to mental problems. Consumer pressure has inspired some meat processors to eliminate these dangerous chemicals from their products. Reading labels will enable you to select foods free of nitrates and nitrites.

Artificial Colors and Flavors. The admirable judicial concept of "innocent until proven guilty" cannot be applied when it comes to foods containing these chemical additives. Some food manufacturers, since they are not required to state the presence of artificial colors and flavors on their products, have package labels which are void of such information. Where possible, it is best to avoid those foods, which more often than not contain such additives: most brands of ice cream, other frozen desserts, dessert and cake mixes, bakery products, oleomargarine, many breakfast cereals, gelatin desserts, candies, chewing gum, jam or jelly, luncheon meats, frankfurters, "kiddie drinks," canned fruit-juice punches and drinks. Many processed cheeses and cheese products, as well as colorfully coated pills (including some vitamin products) also contain these harmful additives and should be avoided where possible.

Label-reading will help to this extent: products free from artificial additives generally proclaim their "innocence" on the package. Try to limit your food purchases to those items whose labels boast of all natural ingredients.

Did that list of suspect foods sound familiar? It should—many that have been named are the ones that should also be avoided because they contain sugar, white flour, hydrogenated fat, or nitrate-nitrite additives. Remember, food is like the little girl with the curl in the middle of her forehead: when it's bad, it's horrid.

Caloric yield in terms of resistance agents—protein, vitamins, and minerals—can be greatly increased through wise food selection. When items from the "foods-to-eat-liberally" list make up the bulk of your diet, you can get up to fifty times more nourishment each day than you might otherwise. To show you how this works, we have chosen an adequate day's menu from the "foods to eat liberally" list and compared its nutritional value to an inadequate menu largely selected from the "foods to avoid" list. The two menus provide an *identical number of calories*, but there all similarity ends.

Let's start with breakfast:

Adequate menu: ½ grapefruit, 2 eggs, 3 oz. ham, 1 slice whole-grain bread with butter, 1 glass of milk.

Inadequate menu: 3 hot cakes with butter and syrup, 1 cup coffee with sugar and cream.

Now let's see how these two breakfasts compare nutritionally:

Nutrients	Adequate Breakfast (700 calories)	Inadequate Breakfast (700 calories)	Adequate: Inadequate Ratio
ascorbic acid (mg.)	50	0.0	50.0:1
nicotinic acid (mg.)	15	0.6	25.0:1
phosphorus (mg.)	760	100	7.6:1
calcium (mg.)	460	65	7.1:1
riboflavin (mg.)	1.07	0.18	5.9:1
protein (gm.)	45	8	5.6:1
iodine (mcg.)	17	4	4.3:1
iron (mg.)	7	2	3.5:1
vitamin A (I.U.)	4200	1400	3.0:1
thiamine (mg.)	0.8	0.4	2.0:1
fat (gm.)	40	30	1.3:1
carbohydrate (gm.)	40	100	0.4:1

Let's follow the same procedure for two sample lunches:

Adequate lunch: 1 bowl vegetable soup, shrimp salad, 1 slice whole-grain bread with butter, 1 glass buttermilk, 1 apple.

Inadequate lunch: 1 ham sandwich, 1 soft drink, 1 piece of pie.

Nutrients	Adequate Lunch (655 calories)	Inadequate Lunch (655 calories)	Adequate: Inadequate Ratio
iodine (mcg.)	34	1.4	24.3:1
ascorbic acid (mg.)	10	1	10.0:1
iron (mg.)	4	0.6	6.7:1
riboflavin (mg.)	0.53	0.1	5.3:1
calcium (mg.)	370	75	4.9:1
vitamin A (I.U.)	1930	420	4.6:1

Nutrients	Adequate Lunch (655 calories)	Inadequate Lunch (655 calories)	Adequate: Inadequate Ratio
phosphorus (mg.)	440	120	3.7:1
thiamine (mg.)	0.26	0.07	3.7:1
protein (gm.)	28	11	2.5:1
fat (gm.)	27	21	1.3:1
nicotinic acid (mg.)	3	2.5	1.2:1
carbohydrate (gm.)	75	105	0.7:1

And then comes dinner. Which of these two meals looks familiar?

Adequate dinner: 4 oz. tomato juice, mixed green salad with vinegar dressing, 6 oz. roast beef, baked potato with 1 square butter, green peas, ½ cantaloupe with 1 oz. cheddar cheese, 1 glass buttermilk.

Inadequate dinner: spaghetti and meat balls, mixed green salad with French dressing, French bread and 1 square butter, French pastry, coffee with sugar and cream.

Nutrients	Adequate Dinner (890 calories)	Inadequate Dinner (890 calories)	Adequate: Inadequate Ratio
ascorbic acid (mg.)	90	10	9.0:1
riboflavin (mg.)	1.4	0.29	4.8:1
iodine (mcg.)	45	11	4.1:1
nicotinic acid (mg.)	16	4.5	3.6:1
calcium (mg.)	600	175	3.4:1
thiamine (mg.)	0.84	0.26	3.2:1
phosphorus (mg.)	860	321	2.7:1
vitamin A (I.U.)	4900	1900	2.6:1

Nutrients	Adequate Dinner (890 calories)	Inadequate Dinner (890 calories)	Adequate: Inadequate Ratio
protein (gm.)	70	28	2.5:1
iron (mg.)	10	4	2.5:1
fat (gm.)	30	40	0.8:1
carbohydrate (gm.)	85	105	0.8:1

You don't have to be a math whiz to see that the "adequate" calories provide up to fifty times more nutritional value than the "inadequate" calories. As the foregoing charts indicate, the "adequate" breakfast provides fifty times as many milligrams of ascorbic acid as the "inadequate" one, twenty-five times the milligrams of nicotinic acid, and so forth down the nutrient list.

Having learned *what* to eat, does it matter *when* and in what combination? Yes. The first meal of the day is critically important. (We'll bet this isn't the first time you've heard *that*.) Breakfast breaks the overnight fast and prepares you for the day's physical and mental exertion. For the hypoglycemic, breakfast is even more essential.

Those people who skip breakfast or eat a skimpy one usually feel a midmorning letdown. Their energy, physical and mental, is certain to be lowered. Ideally, you should get a fourth to a third of your *total* daily nutrients at breakfast. You can't do this on junk foods or those instant breakfast items advertised to be "just as good as" the adequate breakfast menu described.

Contrary to popular belief, between-meal snacking is not necessarily an undesirable habit. Assuming the calorie total remains about the same, it's fine to spread daily food intake over five or six feedings, say, three meals and two or three snacks. Breaking up your food intake into smaller, more frequent "meals" helps stabilize blood-sugar levels and decrease hunger and fatigue. A great many dieters lose weight more easily on five or six feedings a day, and the underweight often gain.

Choose your snack foods carefully. Don't fall into the junk-foods trap. Restrict your nibbling to such foods as nuts, sunflower and other seeds, milk, cheese, fresh fruit, unsweetened fruit or vegetable juices, and raw vegetables. These foods satisfy your body needs, and you will soon lose your craving for all those bubbly, sticky, sugary, or crunchy products normally considered snacks.

Let's assume that you've become a post-psychodietetics eater and that you've closely followed all the advice in the pages of this book. Are you now assured of an adequate supply of all the essential nutrients each day? Perhaps. An *optimum* supply? Not on your life! You still need additional vitamins and minerals, for a number of reasons:

Significant nutritional value is lost as food is processed.

An *excess* of each essential nutrient is desirable as a hedge against malnutrition from primary or secondary dietary deficiencies. An increased requirement for one or more nutrients may be caused by individual biochemistry, psychological stress, surgery, all kinds of diseases, physical inactivity, pollution, aging, medicines by the hundreds, and many other factors too numerous to mention. The food you eat, by itself, simply cannot assure this important nutrient excess.

No one can or will eat optimally 100 percent of the time; so even if food lost no value either when grown, prepared, transported, or served (and it inevitably does), supplements would still be necessary.

When choosing a dietary supplement, remember that the product should provide all the essential vitamins and minerals plus many of the so-called nonessential elements as well. Vitamin-mineral supplements should always be taken *before* or *during* each meal, when the digestive juices are flowing. This assures your having *all* the essential nutrients present at the same time in the digestive tract, a condition essential for optimal growth, maintenance, and repair of your body and brain cells.

How do you choose a vitamin-mineral supplement? Read the

label. A good one, taken with each meal, would supply these quantities of brain-cell nutrients per day:

vitamin A	10,000–25,000 USP Units
vitamin D	1000–2500 USP Units
vitamin E (d-alpha tocopherol)	100–800 I.U.
vitamin C	300–1500 mg.
bioflavonoids	50–300 mg.
vitamin B_1 (thiamin)	10–25 mg.
vitamin B_2 (riboflavin)	10–25 mg.
vitamin B_6 (pyridoxine)	10–25 mg.
vitamin B_{12} (cyanocobalamin)	20–100 mcg.
folic acid	75–100 mcg.
niacin or niacinamide	75–150 mg.
pantothenic acid	50–200 mg.
PABA	25–50 mg.
biotin	25–50 mcg.
choline	100–500 mg.
inositol	100–500 mg.
calcium	250–1000 mg.
phosphorus	100–200 mg.
iron	10–25 mg.
copper	0.5–2 mg.
iodine	0.15 mg.
zinc	2–20 mg.
manganese	2–20 mg.
magnesium	20–300 mg.
potassium	20–40 mg.

Brewer's yeast, desiccated liver, and bone meal are good sources of some B vitamins, of important trace elements not included in the supplement formula, and of as-yet-unidentified nutrients. Yeast and liver are, in addition, excellent protein supplements.

One of the controversial questions of the day is how much

vitamin C and vitamin E should be taken. Since these two nutrients are likely to be on the low side in many supplements, you may have to purchase a separate quantity of each to get *at least* 1000 milligrams of vitamin C and 600–800 International Units of vitamin E daily. Recent evidence indicates that men need 2500 milligrams of vitamin C daily to protect them from the common cold; women need 2000.

Are there inherent dangers in taking large doses of vitamins? Can you take too much of any nutrient? Yes. You can take too much of anything, including water and air. Common sense would dictate that you can take too many vitamins.

The margin of safety is the point to consider. Fortunately, when it comes to vitamins, there is a tremendous margin. The few studies to date which seem to support a vitamin A and vitamin D toxicity potential used fantastically large quantities to demonstrate an ill effect. You'd have to sit down and plan your own demise to take a damaging dosage of these nutrients.

What about a wasteful excess? Vitamin critics often claim that large amounts of vitamin C, for example, are simply urinated away. A number of studies, however, indicate that an excreted overflow is no proof that the vitamin C wasn't needed and used. Moreover, what the body is able to use depends not only upon need, but upon how the nutrient is presented. If you take 1000 milligrams of vitamin C in one dose, you will excrete far more of it than if you break up the same amount in smaller doses spread throughout the day, taken with each meal.

Those suffering from indigestion may need to take a digestant, hydrochloric acid in some form, in addition to a vitamin-mineral supplement. In a study of 3484 patients with gastrointestinal distress, nearly a third did not secrete enough hydrochloric acid in their stomachs to begin the digestive process. (A teaspoon or two of vinegar with each meal will tell you in one day if you do or do not need more acid in your stomach.) If it relieves your indigestion, you need hydrochloric acid. In such a case, consult your doctor. He can prescribe it in a variety of forms. Some symptoms of stomach-acid deficiency are: sore mouth (rawness, burning, dryness) or tongue, cracks or sores at the corners of the lips; a burning sensation in the stomach; feeling full for long periods after eating, especially after meat; noticeable gas in the stomach and intestinal tract. A deficiency of stomach acid, and the malnutrition it causes, may impair mental health, and any existing mental illness may be aggravated.

If you have trouble digesting fat, bile salts and pancreatic enzymes (no prescription needed) will relieve the indigestion in one or two days. The latter also aid in the digestion of carbohydrates and protein.

Where digestive disturbances have existed for some time, or have been caused by antibiotics (which kill useful intestinal microorganisms as well as disease-producing ones), it is often necessary to reinoculate the digestive tract with friendly microbes. A supplement of the microorganism Lactobacillus acidophilus taken with each meal, in liquid, tablet, or capsule form, will help to reestablish a normal microbial population in the digestive tract and aid significantly in relieving indigestion and diarrhea. Buttermilk and yogurt, both sources of Lactobacillus, can be consumed between meals. If you're taking an antibiotic, taking buttermilk or yogurt along with it will keep you from developing a microbe-depleted digestive system.

Constipation or diarrhea can result from a diet deficient in undigestible vegetable fiber, much of which is removed in grain-processing. One to six teaspoonsful of unprocessed wheat bran, taken with each meal, will help to regulate you.

By following the Optimal Diet, you directly affect your intake of essential brain-cell nutrients. In less time than you might have believed possible, many emotional symptoms will diminish, then disappear. You can check your progress by retaking tests provided throughout the book. Hopefully, your new eating habits will eventually enable you to answer no to all the questions listed in Chapter Twelve.

You may wish to check your food choices with the unique food-scoring system introduced by Dr. Jacobson in his booklet, *Nutrition Scoreboard: Your Guide to Better Eating.* He grades the most

commonly consumed foods by assigning ratings ranging from
+200 to -100. His plus-rated foods, for the most part, are those we
recommend as "foods to eat liberally." The foods to which he
assigns a negative value are those we tagged as "foods to avoid."
Here are some examples from each group:

liver	2 oz.	+172
broccoli	3⅓ oz.	+116
cantaloupe	¼	+ 99
broiled fish	3 oz.	+ 40
milk, whole	8 oz.	+ 39
rye bread	2 slices	+ 29
tomato juice	4 oz.	+ 26
peanuts	¼ cup	+ 25
hot dog	1	+ 6
soda pop	12 oz.	- 92
Morton coconut cream pie	¼ pie	- 62
Kool Aid	8 oz.	- 55
Jello	½ cup	- 45
Del Monte vanilla pudding	1	- 43
candy bar	15-cent bar	- 34

The adequate eater is frequently referred to as a "health nut" or
a "food faddist." The real "food faddist," however, is the inadequate eater who is living on empty-calorie junk foods.

Based on the *Nutrition Scoreboard* food ratings, the average diet
of a "nutrition-conscious woman" and a "young food faddist"
would score like this:

• **A Nutrition-Conscious Woman**

Food		Serving	Calories	Food Rating
Breakfast:	Wheat Chex	1 oz.	120	+ 84
	skim milk	8 oz.	90	+ 49
	grapefruit	½	45	+ 45
	coffee	8 oz.	3	0
Snack:	peach	1	35	+ 29
Lunch:	creamed cottage cheese	1 cup	260	+ 68
	tomato	1	40	+ 69
	whole-wheat bread	1 slice	62	+ 13
	Swiss cheese	2 oz.	200	+ 43
	iced tea	8 oz.	3	0
Snack:	peanuts	¼ cup	210	+ 25
Dinner:	boneless chicken breast	2.7 oz.	155	+ 62
	broccoli	3⅓ oz.	26	+116
	enriched egg noodles	0.9 oz.	164	+ 28
	skim milk	8 oz.	90	+ 49
	fruit salad:			
	strawberries	½ cup	28	+ 50
	cantaloupe	¼	45	+ 99
	raisins	1½ oz.	82	+ 13
Totals:			1658	+842

• A Young Food Faddist

Food		Serving	Calories	Food Rating
Breakfast:	Cocoa Krispies	1 oz.	111	+ 38
	whole milk	4 oz.	160	+ 19
	Pop Tarts	2	416	+ 42
Snack:	Cracker Jacks	1 box	74	− 39
Lunch:	hot dog	1	142	+ 6
	bun	1	114	+ 18
	potato chips	¾ oz.	115	+ 8
	Hunts Snack-Pack Pudding	1	238	− 20
	Hi-C drink	6 oz.	89	+ 4
Snack:	ice cream	3 oz.	95	− 18
	Mom's Apple Pie	6 oz.	243	− 40
	soda pop	12 oz.	145	− 92
Dinner:	Swanson Spaghetti and Meatball TV	1	323	+ 80
	soda pop	12 oz.	145	− 92
	chocolate cake	3 oz.	338	− 53
Snack:	Snickers candy bar	1	240	− 23
	soda pop	12 oz.	145	− 92
Totals			3134	−254

Throughout this book, we have told the stories of people with "emotional" problems who were helped by nutritional therapy. The three case histories that follow—selected from our files on more than 15,000 patients who've been helped—are different. Here, we're going to share with you the precise nutrient changes and their results: the scientific proof in the psychodietetic pudding.

In each case, psychological tests and seven-day computerized diet analyses were done, both *before* putting the patients on the Optimal Diet and three to six months afterward.

Case #14937. This fifteen-year-old boy was suffering several psychological disturbances when we first saw him: he worried a great deal; his feelings were easily hurt; he got upset at the slightest criticism; he was on guard, even with close friends; he was easily upset or irritated. In his words, "little annoyances get on my nerves and make me angry, and I get angry when someone tells me what to do." He also reported finding most people both annoying and irritating.

Maybe he sounds like your own teen-ager, or the Dennis the Menace next door.

After putting this boy on the Optimal Diet, we analyzed his before-and-after nutrient changes and found that they ranged from an increase of 825 percent to a decrease of 78 percent. Of the seventeen essential brain-cell nutrients, we analyzed thirteen; of these, eleven increased and six more than doubled.

Here is his actual record of nutrient change.

nutrient	percentage change
(essential brain-cell nutrients are starred)	
1. vitamin E	+825
* 2. vitamin B_1	+315
* 3. vitamin B_2	+307
4. iron	+291
* 5. vitamin B_3	+282
* 6. vitamin B_{12}	+197
* 7. pantothenic acid	+140
8. % polyunsaturated to saturated fat	+133
* 9. vitamin B_6	+129
10. unrefined carbohydrates	+ 69
11. vitamin A	+ 57
12. total carbohydrate	+ 43
*13. vitamin C	+ 41
14. polyunsaturated fatty acids	+ 33
*15. threonine	+ 33

nutrient	percentage change
16. animal protein	+ 21
17. refined carbohydrates	+ 13
*18. potassium	+ 9
*19. magnesium	+ 6
20. calcium	+ 3
*21. tryptophane	+ 1
22. total protein	− 12
23. phosphorus	− 13
24. calories	− 14
*25. lysine	− 21
26. iso-leucine	− 21
27. valine	− 25
*28. iodine	− 28
29. methionine	− 29
30 sodium	− 42
31. vegetable protein	− 45
32. fat	− 47
33. leucine	− 56
34. phenylalanine	− 78

His before-and-after psychological condition? He went from eight complaints to *zero* complaints in less than six months.

Case #14904. When this suburban housewife first signed in, she was suffering from forty-one psychological complaints and was a prime candidate for psychoanalysis, tranquilizers, and other medications.

Here is the way she described herself:

"I'm nervous, shaky, my work falls to pieces whenever anyone is watching me or talks to me. I'm confused, I'm afraid when alone, usually unhappy and depressed, have frequent crying spells—I'm always miserable and blue, and often wish I were dead and away from it all. Worrying gets me down, and I'm shy and sensitive. Even my best friends consider me a touchy person, and people usually misunderstand me. I stay on guard all the time and always do things on sudden impulse. I usually feel as if I am ready to go to pieces at a moment's notice, have a violent temper, often shake and tremble because I'm so constantly keyed up and jittery. Sudden noises or movements frighten me and leave me weak or shaky. Many a night I pop awake after a frightening dream, and I frequently find myself, even during the day, scared for no good reason."

Was she suffering "midlife crisis"? Seeking her "identity"? Aimless and lost because of her life situation? Our analysis revealed that she was just eating badly. We analyzed her nutrient intake before and after she had been on the Optimal Diet; it varied from an increase of 253 percent to a decrease of 80 percent. Thirteen of the seventeen essential brain-cell nutrients were included in this analysis. All thirteen increased, five of them by more than 100 percent.

nutrient	percentage change
(essential brain-cell nutrients are starred)	
* 1. vitamin B_{12}	+253
* 2. vitamin C	+200
* 3. vitamin B_3	+179
* 4. vitamin B_1	+137
* 5. vitamin B_6	+135
. 6. total protein	+ 87
* 7. magnesium	+ 83
* 8. vitamin B_2	+ 72
9. iron	+ 63
*10. potassium	+ 51
*11. iodine	+ 48
12. fat	+ 46
13. animal protein	+ 43

nutrient	percentage change
*14. lysine	+ 36
15. methionine	+ 29
16. vitamin A	+ 22
*17. pantothenic acid	+ 20
18. phosphorus	+ 20
19. vitamin D	+ 19
20. iso-leucine	+ 18
21. phenylalanine	+ 14
22. leucine	+ 12
*23. tryptophane	+ 12
*24. threonine	+ 12
25. valine	+ 11
26. refined carbohydrates	+ 11
27. calcium	+ 9
28. calories	+ 7
29. total carbohydrate	− 3
30. sodium	− 10
31. vegetable protein	− 13
32. vitamin E	− 16
33. unrefined carbohydrates	− 19
34. polyunsaturated fatty acids	− 70
35. % polyunsaturated to saturated fat	− 80

After years of escalating mental torture, our patient enjoyed almost complete emotional recovery in *less than one year*. Her psychological complaints were reduced to ten, most of a minor nature, and there is every reason to believe that she will someday be down to an emotionally stable zero if she sticks to the Optimal Diet.

Case #14935. This was a fifty-year-old man, set in his ways, and particularly hard to convince that changing his diet would change his disposition—which, he admitted, was "rotten."

"I'm basically shy and extremely sensitive," he told us, "yet I know I have a violent temper. I'm always nervous and indecisive under pressure—I sweat profusely, feel shaky, and sometimes shake literally."

He went along with our program, skeptical every step of the way. His before-and-after intake of specific nutrients ranged from an increase of 650 percent to a decrease of 50 percent.

Again, thirteen of the seventeen essential brain-cell nutrients were included in our analysis. Ten of the thirteen increased, and six more than doubled.

nutrient	percentage change
(essential brain-cell nutrients are starred)	
1. vitamin E	+650
2. vitamin D	+507
* 3. vitamin B_1	+505
* 4. vitamin B_2	+438
5. vitamin A	+416
6. iron	+386
* 7. vitamin B_{12}	+335
* 8. vitamin B_3	+317
* 9. vitamin B_6	+267
*10. pantothenic acid	+193
*11. magnesium	+ 60
12. % polyunsaturated to saturated fat	+ 57
13. polyunsaturated fatty acids	+ 33
*14. vitamin C	+ 19
*15. potassium	+ 16
*16. tryptophane	+ 12
17. refined carbohydrates	0
18. fat	− 8
19. calories	− 12
20. total carbohydrate	− 12

nutrient	percentage change
21. unrefined carbohydrates	− 15
22. phosphorus	− 17
23. animal protein	− 17
24. calcium	− 17
25. valine	− 22
26. total protein	− 23
27. iso-leucine	− 28
28. sodium	− 30
29. phenylalanine	− 31
*30. threonine	− 33
31. leucine	− 34
32. methionine	− 36
*33. lysine	− 36
*34. iodine	− 38
35. vegetable protein	− 50

No one was more surprised than our patient when he found that he no longer became easily upset or irritated, that he had lost his violent temper, and that he could talk to his boss without dissolving into fearful tremors and shakes.

Most behavioral scientists would scoff at the idea that fifty years of "learned behavior" can be reversed in just a few months by a mere change in diet; yet this case, like all the cases in our files, can be verified.

Similar dramas take place every day; *you can write the next scenario yourself.*

Winston Churchill once advised the Duke of Windsor: "If you have an important point to make, don't try to be subtle or clever. Use a pile driver. Hit the point once. Then come back and hit it again. Then hit it a third time—a tremendous whack."

One more time then: all our research, everything in our clinical experience over the past twenty-five years, has convinced us that you can improve your emotional state by improving your nutrition: by making sure that every body cell receives optimal amounts of every essential nutrient.

Psychodietetics has told you why, shown you how. The next whack is up to you.

Appendix A

Although the consumption of megadoses of vitamin B_3 is quite safe, there are several contraindications and annoying side effects. They are effectively summarized in a useful booklet, *Megavitamin Therapy*, which is published by Kárpát Publishing Company, P.O. Box 5348, Cleveland, Ohio 44101. Anyone on megavitamins should order this informative booklet. According to *Megavitamin Therapy* these precautions should be observed:

• **Contraindications**

Peptic ulcer or hyper-acidity patients should observe the diet and medication prescribed by their physicians, and if they cannot tolerate niacin, should use it with antacids; or they can use other preparations like buffered niacin or niacinamide.

Diabetics may need more insulin when they take niacin, though not all diabetics react this way.

High blood pressure patients who use Reserpine type medications may experience nausea and considerable drop in blood pressure, when using high dosages of niacin. This might not be dangerous, but could be very inconvenient.

Liver function tests might show false indications for a person on niacin. Therefore, niacin should be discontinued for a week before this or other sensitive tests [like the glucose tolerance test] are taken. *Smoking* also disturbs glucose tolerance tests.

192

- **Side Effects**

Vitamin B_3: *Niacin*, but not niacinamide, causes *flushing* at the beginning. Your skin turns pink, as though you had a sunburn. You might feel your skin tighten and you may have some prickling feeling or itching. This flush might start almost immediately, or hours after you take the pill, and at the beginning it might last for a few hours. Some people like it; others, especially children, cannot tolerate it. If you drink a glass of cold milk after taking the tablets it reduces the flush. Or take niacin with the solid part of your meal. Regulate your schedule so that there is little flushing in public. Your physician can prescribe 4 mg. Periactin, but take this only when you wish to eliminate flush or other side effects. Even if you got accustomed to niacin and do not flush any more, it starts again if you neglect taking niacin for a few days and then take it again. If you cannot get accustomed to it, change to niacinamide, which does not cause flush. Neither flush nor the other side effects are dangerous, but might be very inconvenient to some people.

Flush is more intensive if niacin is taken on an empty stomach, or with a hot drink, and is lessened if taken after meals or with cold milk. When Periactin is used to alleviate flush, the best time to give it is a few minutes after the flush begins. When flush is very inconvenient, slow-release forms of niacin can be prescribed though they are more expensive.

Dryness of skin, or *increased brownish color* may be caused by niacin and nicotinamide. These are harmless and disappear in time.

About five people out of 100 get *headaches*. If this occurs, switch to slow release niacin or niacinamide.

A few people develop *nausea* and rarely even *vomiting*. Vomiting or nausea may increase during influenza infection. These can be remedied by Periactin or by using buffered niacin, or niacinamide.

Niacinamide produces vomiting only if the dosage is too high. You can find out the optimal dosage for you by raising the dosage by one gram until vomiting occurs. Then reduce it by one gram. This is your optimal dosage.

Soft stools, *diarrhea*, and *foul-smelling stools* are possible side effects, but generally disappear when treatment is discontinued and do not appear again when treatment is resumed.

If *skin rash* develops, it can be cured by taking 4 mg. Periactin with the niacin, when needed.

In some rare cases, a drop in blood pressure, insomnia, or depression may accompany the use of niacin or niacinamide, and a physician should be consulted.

Hypoglycemia patients are generally benefited by niacin, but *diabetic* ones may need to increase their insulin dosage.

Gout may be precipitated by niacin according to some authors, although Dr. Hoffer says that while the uric acid level may increase in some subjects, gout is not aggravated or produced.

Allergic reactions might occur, due not to niacin but to the filler [starch, etc.] used to make the tablets. In this case, products of another company should be tried out, because they might use a different kind of filler that does not activate the allergy.

Appendix B

For additional information, the following addresses will prove valuable.

For a personalized nutrient analysis of your diet:

Dicalator, P.O. Box 3217, Olympic Station, Beverly Hills, California 90212.

Dietronics, c/o Hanson Research Corporation, P.O. Box 35, 19727 Bahama Street, Northridge, California 91324.

More comprehensive questionnaires:

The Hoffer-Osmond Test for Schizophrenia. Bell Therapeutic Supplies, Inc., 382 Schenck Avenue, Brooklyn, New York 11207.

Health Appraisal Indicator (for hypoglycemia). Dr. John F. Bumpus, 7400 West Fourteenth Street, Denver, Colorado 80215.

General Health Questionnaire. Dr. David P. Goldberg, c/o General Practice Research Unit, de Crespigny Park, London, S.E. 5, England.

Symptometer. Kárpát Publishing Company, P.O. Box 5348, Cleveland, Ohio 44101.

Special problem organizations:

The American Schizophrenia Association, 56 West 45th Street, Suite 805, New York, New York 10036.

National Council on Alcoholism, 2 Park Avenue, New York, New York 10016.

Alcoholics Anonymous General Service Office, P.O. Box 459, Grand Central Station, New York, New York 10017.

Schizophrenics Anonymous International, Box 913, Saskatoon, Saskatchewan, Canada.

Hypoglycemia Foundation, Inc., P.O. Box 25, Fleetwood, Mount Vernon, New York 10552.

A referral list of active members of the Academy of Orthomolecular Psychiatry:

David Hawkins, M.D., 1691 Northern Boulevard, Manhasset, Long Island, New York 10030, or Alan Cott, M.D., 303 Lexington Avenue, New York, New York 10016.

A referral list of nutritionally oriented doctors:

The International Academy of Metabology, 2236 Suree Ellen Lane, Altadena, Califorina 91001 and International College of Applied Nutrition, Box 386, La Habra, California 90631

Other books:

New Hope for Incurable Diseases, Exposition Press, Inc., 50 Jericho Turnpike, Jericho, New York 11753, or Arco Publishing Company, Inc., 219 Park Avenue South, New York, New York 11753.

Diet and Disease, Rodale Press, Book Division, Emmaus, Pennsylvania 18049.

Megavitamin Therapy in Orthomolecular Psychiatry, Kárpát Publishing Company, P.O. Box 5348, Cleveland, Ohio 44101.

Megavitamin Therapy and the Drug Wipeout Syndrome, Do It Now Foundation, P.O. Box 5115, Phoenix, Arizona 85010.

Nutrition Scoreboard: Your Guide to Better Eating, Center for

Science in the Public Interest, 1779 Church Street, N.W., Washington, D.C. 20036.

The Physiological Effects of Wheat Germ Oil on Humans in Exercise, Charles C. Thomas, Publisher, Springfield, Illinois.

The Pulse Test, Arco Publishing Company, Inc., 219 Park Avenue South, New York, New York 10003.

Appendix C

The Hypoglycemia Diet, a modification of the *Seale Harris Diet* for hyperinsulinism, as developed by Dr. Harry M. Salzer, 6056 Montgomery Road, Cincinnati, Ohio 45213.

Immediately on Arising: 4 to 6 ounces orange juice, frozen or fresh; or one medium orange. (Orange juice or orange allowed only once a day on arising.)

Breakfast: Fruit or 4 ounces juice; 1 or 2 eggs with or without two slices of bacon or ham; *only one* slice of any bread or toast but with plenty of butter or oleomargarine; beverage.

2 Hours after Breakfast: 8 ounces juice or milk.

Lunch: Meat, fish, cheese or eggs; salad (large servings of lettuce, tomato, or Waldorf salad with mayonnaise or French dressing); vegetables if desired; *only one* slice of any bread with butter or oleomargarine; dessert; beverage.

2 or 3 Hours after Lunch: 8 ounces milk.

1 Hour before Dinner: 4 ounces juice.

Dinner: Soup if desired (not thickened with flour); *liberal* portion of meat, fish, or poultry; vegetables; *only one* slice of bread if desired but with plenty of butter or oleomargarine; salad; dessert; beverage.

Every 2 Hours until Retiring: 8 ounces milk and/or a small handful of nuts or 1 or 2 saltines but must be with cheese or peanut butter.

If Wakeful during Night: Eat a high protein-snack. Meat, or milk, or nuts, or 4 ounces of allowable juice may be taken hourly through the day if underweight or if symptoms are severe.

• **Food and Drink Allowed**

Allowable Vegetables: Fresh, frozen or canned: artichoke, aspara-gus, avocado, beets, black-eyed peas, broccoli, brussels sprouts, cabbage, cauliflower, carrots, celery, corn, cucumbers, eggplant, garlic, kale, lentils, lettuce, lima beans, mushrooms, okra, onions, peas, peppers, pumpkin, radishes, sauerkraut, soy beans, spinach, squash, string beans, sunflower seeds, tomatoes, turnips, water-cress. (Corn, lima beans, lentils, and peas are least desirable.)

Allowable Fruits: Fresh or cooked or unsweetened frozen or canned: apples, apricots, berries, cherries, fresh coconut, grape-fruit, kumquats, lemons, limes, mango, melon, papayas, peaches, pears, pineapple, and tangerines—with or without cream *but without sugar.* Sweeten with artificial (low-calorie) sweetener if desired.

Allowable Juice: The following if unsweetened: apple, grapefruit (orange juice or orange only on arising), pineapple, tomato, vege-table, Vegemato, V-8. Knox gelatin may be added for protein.

Allowable Beverages: Above juices, dietetic carbonated drinks *except cola,* creamed or plain buttermilk, Kaffir tea (obtainable at health food stores), milk, vichy, Fizzies, Fresca.

Allowable Desserts: Fruit, unsweetened gelatin, Dezerta fruit flavors, and the following dietetic products: candy (except choco-late), gum, fruits, ice cream, jelly or puddings—sweetened with artificial sweetener but not sugar, syrup or honey. Dietetic maple syrup is permitted.

• **Absolutely None of the Following**

Sugar, honey, candy including chocolate; other sweets such as cake, chewing gum, Jello, pastries, pie, puddings, sweet custard, sweet jelly or marmalade, and ice cream.

Caffeine: ordinary coffee and even coffee substitutes such as Sanka or Decaf; tea, beverages containing caffeine such as Coca Cola, Pepsi Cola, other cola drinks, Ovaltine, Postum, hot choco-late.

No ordinary carbonated drinks. *No grape, prune, or other juices than those listed above.*

Bananas, dates, dried fruits, figs, grapes, persimmons, plums, prunes, raisins.

Macaroni, navy and kidney beans, noodles, potatoes, rice, cereals, spaghetti, ravioli.

Beer, cocktails, cordials, wines.

Medications containing caffeine such as Anacin, A.P.C., A.S.A. Compound, B.C., Caffergot, Coricidin, Excedrin, Empirin Compound, Fiorinal, Four Way Cold Tablets, Salfayne, Stanback, Trigesic, Darvon Compound. *(Plain aspirin or bufferin permitted.)*

Read the label on every can of juice, fruit, vegetable, meat, and other products. Select only those containing no syrup, honey, or sugar. These can be found at the dietetic counters in all large markets.

References

CHAPTER ONE

Blaine, T. R. *Mental Health Through Nutrition.* 1969. New York: The Citadel Press.

Bolton, R. *Aggression and Hypoglycemia Among the Qolla: A Study in Psychobiological Anthropology.* A paper presented at the 71st annual meeting of the American Anthropological Association in Toronto, Canada, 1 December 1972. A revision of this paper is to appear in *Ethnology* 12, 1973.

Dubos, R. J. *Mirage of Health.* 1959. New York: Harper and Brothers.

Eccleston, D. The Biochemistry of Human Moods. *New Scientist,* 18–19, 4 January 1973.

Hawkins, D. R., and Pauling, L. *Orthomolecular Psychiatry: Treatment of Schizophrenia.* 1973. San Francisco: W. H. Freeman and Company.

Hoffer, A., and Osmond, H. *How to Live with Schizophrenia.* 1966. New Hyde Park, New York: University Books.

Lasagna, L. *The Doctor's Dilemma.* 1962. New York: Harper and Brothers.

Lindner, R., and Seliger, R. *Handbook of Correctional Psychology.* 1947. New York: Philosophical Library.

May, J. M. The Ecology of Human Disease. *Annals of the New York Academy of Sciences* 84: #17, 789–794, 8 December 1960.

Nichols, J. D. *Please, Doctor, Do Something.* 1972. Atlanta, Texas: Natural Food Associates

Rosenfeld, C. Nutritional Guidance Can Forestall Broken Marriages. *New Medical Materia* 51: #8, 51–52, August 1962.

United States Department of Health, Education, and Welfare, National Center for Health Statistics, Series 11, Number 37. *Selected Symptoms of Psychological Distress, United States.* 1970. Washington, D.C., United States Government Printing Office.

Williams, R. J. *Biochemical Individuality: The Basis for the Genetotrophic Concept.* 1956. New York: John Wiley and Sons.

Williams, R. J. *Nutrition Against Disease: Environmental Protection.* 1971. New York: Pitman Publishing Company.

CHAPTER TWO

Cheraskin, E., Ringsdorf, W. M., Jr., and Clark, J. W. *Diet and Disease.* 1968. Emmaus, Pennsylvania: Rodale Books, Inc.

Cheraskin, E., and Ringsdorf, W. M., Jr. What Does the Dental Family Eat? A Study of Refined Carbohydrate Consumption. *Journal of the Alabama Dental Association* 56: #1, 32–39, January 1972.

Clark, J. W., Cheraskin, E., and Ringsdorf, W. M., Jr. *Diet and the Periodontal Patient.* 1970. Springfield: Charles C. Thomas.

Dubos, R. *Mirage of Health.* 1959. New York: Harper and Brothers.

Dubos, R. *Pasteur and Modern Science.* 1960. Garden City: Anchor Books, Inc.

Galdston, I. *Beyond the Germ Theory: The Role of Deprivation and Stress in Health and Disease.* 1954. New York: Health Education Council.

Galdston, I. *Medicine in Transition.* 1965. Chicago: The University of Chicago Press.

Garrison, F. H. *An Introduction to the History of Medicine.* 4th ed. 1929. Philadelphia: W. B. Saunders Company.

Harte, R. A., and Chow, B. Dietary Interrelationships. pp. 534–544. In Wohl, M. G., and Goodhart, R. S. *Modern Nutrition in Health and Disease.* 3rd ed. 1964. Philadelphia: Lea and Febiger.

King, L. S. *The Growth of Medical Thought.* 1963. Chicago: The University of Chicago Press.

Lewis, H. R., and Lewis, M. E. *Psychosomatics: How Your Emotions Can Damage Your Health.* 1972. New York: The Viking Press, Inc.

National Dairy Council. Functions and Interrelationships of Vitamins. *Dairy Council Digest* 43: #5, September–October 1972.

Pauling, L. Orthomolecular Psychiatry. *Science* 160: #3825, 265–271, 19 April 1968.

Watson, E. Caution: Living May Be Hazardous to Your Health. *Los Angeles West Magazine*, pp. 6–9, 16 July 1972.

Williams, R. J. *Nutrition Against Disease*. 1971. New York: Pitman Publishing Company.

Medical Tribune Report, Washington Bureau. U.S. Figures Show Mental Illnesses Cost the Public $20 Billion in 1966. *Medical Tribune and Medical News* 9: #21, 3, 11 March 1968.

Medicine's Week. $1,000-a-Day Hospital Rooms Seen. *American Medical News*, 4 May 1970.

Milner, G. Ascorbic Acid in Chronic Psychiatric Patients: A Controlled Trial. *British Journal of Psychiatry* 109: #459, 294–299, March 1963.

Murphy, W. B. Some Things You Might Not Know about the Foods Served to Children. *Nutrition Today* 7: #5, 34–35, September–October 1972.

Pauling, L. C. The New Medicine? *Nutrition Today* 7: #5, 18–23, September–October 1972.

Schroeder, H. A. Losses of Vitamins and Trace Minerals Resulting from Processing and Preservation of Foods. *The American Journal of Clinical Nutrition* 24: #5, 562–573, May 1971.

Toepfer, E. W., Polansky, M. M., Eheart, J. F., Slover, H. T., Morris, E. R., Hepburn, F. N., and Quackenbuch, F. W. Nutrient Composition of Selected Wheats and Wheat Products. XI. Summary. *Cereal Chemistry* 49: #2, 173–186, March–April 1972.

Ubell, E. Too Much Too Late. *Prevention* 21: #9, 57–63, September 1969.

United States Bureau of the Census. *Statistical Abstract of the United States 1971*. Washington, D.C.

United States Department of Agriculture, Agricultural Research Service. *Dietary Levels of Households in the United States, Spring 1965*. ARS 62–17, January 1968.

United States Department of Commerce. *United States Industrial Outlook 1972 with Projections to 1980*. 1972. Washington, D.C.

United States Department of Health, Education, and Welfare, National Center for Health Statistics, Series 11, Number 37. *Selected Symptoms of Psychological Distress, United States*. 1970. Washington, D.C.

United States Department of Health, Education, and Welfare, National Center for Health Statistics, Series 10, Number 72. *Current Estimates from the Health Interview Survey*. 1972. Washington, D.C.

United States Department of Health, Education, and Welfare. *Health Resources Statistics, 1971.* DHEW Publication #[HSM] 72-1509. 1972. Washington, D.C.

United States Department of Health, Education, and Welfare, National Center for Health Statistics, Series 10, Numbers 5, 13, 25, 37, and 43. *Current Estimates from the Health Interview Survey.* 1964-1968. Washington, D.C.

Wade, C. *Emotional Health and Nutrition.* 1971. New York: Award Books.

Washington Star-News, Monday 6 August 1973. Porter, S. Your Money's Worth.

Williams, R. J. *Nutrition Against Disease.* 1971. New York: Pitman Publishing Corporation.

Williams, R. J. Should the Science-Based Food Industry Be Expected to Advance? Paper presented to the National Academy of Sciences, 21 October 1970.

Yudkin, J. *Sweet and Dangerous.* 1972. New York: Peter H. Wyden, Inc.

CHAPTER THREE

Bruch, H. *Eating Disorders.* 1973. New York: Basic Books, Inc.

Consumer Guide. Food: The Brand Name Game; Vol. 63. August 1974.

Consumer Guide. Rating the Diets; Vol. 53. April 1974.

Fredericks, C. *Eating Right for You.* 1972. New York: Grosset and Dunlap.

Fredericks, C. *Food Facts and Fallacies.* 1965. New York: Galahad Books.

Good Housekeeping, March, 1973. Start to Shape Up Now With Keep-Trim and Slim-Down Diet Plan, 120-125.

Solomon, N. *The Truth About Weight Control.* 1971. New York: Stein and Day Publishers.

Stein, M. An Opinion: Dieting to Disaster. *Mademoiselle,* January 1974.

CHAPTER FOUR

Adams, R., and Murray, F. *Body, Mind and the B Vitamins.* 1972. New York: Larchmont Books.

Alsleben, H. R. What Alcohol Will Do to You. *The Answer* 1: #1, 2-4, 19, November 1971.

American Business Man's Research Foundation. *Report on Alcohol.* Fall and Winter 1971. Elinhurst, Illinois 60126.

A Way of Life: Alcoholics Anonymous. Five Points Group [A.A.], Birmingham, Alabama. 1945.

Bardin, J. Visualizing America's Alcoholism. *Today's Health* 50: #10, 7, October 1972.

Brayton, R. G., Stokes, P. E., Schwartz, M. S., and Louria, D. B. Effect of Alcohol and Various Diseases on Leukocyte Mobilization, Phagocytosis and Intracellular Bacterial Killing. *New England Journal of Medicine* 282: #2, 123–128, 15 January 1970.

Cheraskin, E., and Ringsdorf, W. M., Jr. *New Hope for Incurable Diseases.* 1971. Jericho, New York: Exposition Press, Inc.

Criteria Committee, National Council on Alcoholism. Criteria for the Diagnosis of Alcoholism. *American Journal of Psychiatry* 129: #2, 127–135, August 1972.

Editorial. Alcoholism. *The Alcoholism Digest* 1: #1, August 1972.

Editorial. Bad News for Social Drinkers. *Up Look* 1: #1, 1971. Action Center, P.O. Box 901, San Diego, California 92112.

Enzomedic Laboratories, Inc. *Alcohol: Who is Allergic.* 1967. 126 S.W. 157th Street, Seattle, Washington 98166.

Flemming, E. D., Lewis, J. S., and Murtha, W. E. *The Alcoholism Report* 1: #1, 27 October 1972.

Geller, I. Ethanol Preference in the Rat as a Function of Photoperiod. *Science* 173: #3995, 456–459, 30 July 1971.

Goodwin, D. W. Is Alcoholism Hereditary? A Review and Critique. *Archives of General Psychiatry* 25: #6, 545–549, December 1971.

Greenwald, H. *Decision Therapy.* 1973. New York: Peter H. Wyden, Publisher.

Hall, A. You Can Now Predict Whether or Not You Will Become an Alcoholic. *Midnight* 19: #28, 21, 22 January 1973.

Hawkins, D. R., from Wilson, Bill. *The Vitamin B-3 Therapy: A Third Communication to A.A.'s Physicians.* January 1971. N.N.M.H.C., P.O. Box 125, Oyster Bay, New York 11771.

Iber, F. L. In Alcoholism, the Liver Sets the Pace. *Nutrition Today* 6: #1, 2–9, January–February 1971.

If You Are a Professional, A.A. Wants to Work with You. Alcoholics Anonymous World Service, Inc., P.O. Box 459, Grand Central Station, New York, New York 10017.

Is A.A. for You? Twelve Questions You Can Answer. Alcoholics Anonymous World Service, Inc., Box 459, Grand Central Station, New York, New York 10017.

Mann, M. *New Primer on Alcoholism.* 1958. New York: Rinehart and Company, Inc.

Medical News. High Carbohydrate Diet Affects Rat's Alcohol Intake. *Journal of the American Medical Association* 212: #6, 976, 11 May 1970.

Megavitamins, New Hope for the Mentally Ill. *Consumer's Digest.* November/December 1973.

Metz, R., Berger, S., and Mako, M. Potentiation of the Plasma Insulin Response to Glucose by Prior Administration of Alcohol: An Apparent Islet-Priming Effect. *Diabetes* 18: #8, 517–522, August 1969.

Moskow, H. A., Pennington, R. C., and Knisely, M. H. Alcohol, Sludge, and Hypoxic Areas of Nervous System, Liver and Heart. *Microvascular Research* 1: #2, 174–185, October 1968.

Rayjon Associates. *The Alcoholic's Devils, Doctors, and Drugs.* Room 1905, 445 Park Avenue, New York, New York 10022.

Register, V. D., Marsh, S. R., Thurston, C. T., Fields, B. J., Horning, M. C., Hardinge, M. G., and Sanchez, A. Influence of Nutrients on Intake of Alcohol. *Journal of the American Dietetic Association* 61: #2, 159–162, August 1972.

Rodale, J. I. *Rodale's System for Mental Power and Natural Health.* 1968. Emmaus, Pennsylvania: Rodale Press.

Rodale, R. Polluted Rats Turn to Drink. *Rodale's Health Bulletin* 8: #18, 2, 25 July 1970.

Rouse, K. A. *Detour Alcoholism Ahead.* Kemper Insurance, 4750 Sheridan Road, Chicago, Illinois 60640.

Shearer, L. Intelligence Report: Your Heart and Alcohol. *Parade,* 24 June 1973.

Smith, R. F., from Wilson, Bill. *The Vitamin B-3 Therapy: A Second Communication to A.A.'s Physicians.* January 1970. P.O. Box 451, Bedford Hills, New York 10507.

Smith, R. F., from Wilson, Bill. *The Vitamin B-3 Therapy: A Third Communication to A.A.'s Physicians.* January 1971. N.N.M.H.C., P.O. Box 125, Oyster Bay, New York 11771.

Swift, P. Keeping Up with Youth. *Parade,* 14, 16 July 1972.

Williams, R. J. *Alcoholism: The Nutritional Approach.* 1959. Austin: University of Texas Press.

Williams, R. J. *Nutrition Against Disease.* 1971. New York: Pitman Publishing Corporation.

CHAPTER FIVE

American Schizophrenia Association. *What You Should Know about Schizophrenia.* 1965. Seventh Printing, March 1968.

Ananth, J. V., Ban, T. A., and Lehman, H. E. *Potentiation of Therapeutic Effects of Nicotinic Acid by Pyridoxine in Chronic Schizophrenics.* Douglas Hospital, 6875 La Salle Boulevard, Verdun, Quebec, Canada. Supported in part by Public Health Service Research Grant MH–05202–04 from U.S. Department of Health, Education and Welfare.

Back to Reality the Megavitamin Way. *Medical World News,* 24 September 1971. Reprinted by the Huxley Institute for Biosocial Research, Suite 805, 56 West 45th Street, New York, New York 10036.

Better Health Center, 5629 State Road, Cleveland, Ohio 44134. *Symptometer with Symptoscale.* From *Megavitamin Therapy in Orthomolecular Psychiatry.* Tenth edition. Kárpát Publishing Company, Post Office Box 5348, Cleveland, Ohio 44101.

Blaine, T. *Mental Health Through Nutrition.* 1969. Secaucus, New Jersey: Citadel Press.

Canadian Schizophrenia Foundation. *Doctors Speak on the Ortho-Molecular Approach: A Modern Treatment for Schizophrenia and Allied Disorders,* A. Hoffer, M.D., Ph.D.; Humphry Osmond, M.R.C.S., D.P.M.; Allan Cott, M.D.; Jack Ward, M.D.; David Hawkins, M.D.; R. G. Green, M.D.; Bella Kowalson, M.D.

Cancro, R. *The Schizophrenic Syndrome.* Volume 1. 1971. New York: Brunner/Mazel.

Cheraskin, E., and Ringsdorf, W. M., Jr. *New Hope for Incurable Diseases.* 1971. Jericho, New York: Exposition Press, Inc.

Cott, A. *Orthomolecular Treatment: A Biochemical Approach to Treatment of Schizophrenia.* A publication of the American Schizophrenia Association, 56 West 45th Street, New York, New York 10036.

Dohan, F. C., and Grasberger, J. C. Relapsed Schizophrenics: Earlier Discharge from the Hospital after Cereal-Free, Milk-Free Diet. *American Journal of Psychiatry* 130: #6, 685–688, June 1973.

Galton, L. *Why Young Adults Crack Up* [Copyright 1967 by Family Circle, Inc., reprinted by permission]. American Schizophrenia Foundation.

Hawkins, D. R., and Pauling, L. *Orthomolecular Psychiatry: Treatment of Schizophrenia.* 1973. San Francisco, California: W. H. Freeman and Company.

Hawkins, D. R., from Wilson, Bill. *The Vitamin B-3 Therapy: A Third Communication to A.A.'s Physicians.* 1971. N.N.M.H.C., P.O. Box 125, Oyster Bay, New York 11771.

Hoffer, A. *Treatment of Schizophrenia with Nicotinic Acid or Nicotinamide.* October 1965. Kirkman Laboratories, Inc., 934 N.E. 25th Avenue, Portland, Oregon 97208.

Hoffer, A., and Osmond, H. *How to Live with Schizophrenia.* 1966. New Hyde Park, New York: University Books.

Kaplan, A. R. *Genetic Factors in "Schizophrenia."* 1972. Springfield, Illinois: Charles C. Thomas

Letters to the Editor: Mailbag. Schizophrenia and Megavitamins. *Prevention* 24: #11, 197–198, November 1972.

The Organic Side of Mental Illness. *Science News* 104: #4, 61, 28 July 1973.

Pfeiffer, C. C., Ward, J., El-Meligi, M., and Cott, A. *The Schizophrenias: Yours and Mine.* 1970. New York, New York: Pyramid Books.

Pollin, W. The Pathogenesis of Schizophrenia. *Archives of General Psychiatry* 27: #7, 29–37, July 1972.

Shields, Jr., and Gottesman I. I. *The Genetic Basis for Schizophrenia.* Orthomolecular Psychiatry 2: #1, 2–13, First & Second Quaters, 1973.

Wyatt, R. J., Murphy, D. L., Belmaker, R., Cohen, S., Donnelly, C. H., and Pollin, W. Reduced Monoamine Oxidase Activity in Platelets: A Possible Genetic Marker for Vulnerability to Schizophrenia. *Science* 179: #4076, 916–918, 2 March 1973.

CHAPTER SIX

Abrahamson, E. M. *Body, Mind and Sugar.* 1971. Elmhurst, New York: Pyramid Books.

Adams, R., and Murray, F. *Megavitamin Therapy.* 1973. New York: Larchmont Books.

Adrenal Metabolic Research Society. *Hypoglycemia and Me?* Thirteenth Printing. September 1970. Hypoglycemia Foundation, Inc., P.O. Box 25, Fleetwood, Mount Vernon, New York 10552.

Anderson, J. W., and Herman, R. H. Classification of Reactive Hypoglycemia. *American Journal of Clinical Nutrition* 22: #5, 646–650, May 1969.

Anthony, D., Dippe, S., Hofeldt, F. D., Davis, J. W., and Forsham, P. H.

Personality Disorder and Reactive Hypoglycemia: A Quantitative Study. *Diabetes* 22: #9, 664–675, September 1973.

Blaine, T. J. *Mental Health through Nutrition*. 1969. Secaucus, New Jersey: The Citadel Press.

Christian, D. G. Drug Interference with Laboratory Blood Chemistry Determinations. *American Journal of Clinical Pathology* 54: #1, 118–142, July 1970.

Cole, W. Hypoglycemia: Shortage of Body Fuel. *Today's Health* [published by the American Medical Association] 46: #11, November 1968.

Crofford, O. B., and Graber, A. L. Symptomatic Hypoglycemia in Adults: A Protocol for Clinical and Laboratory Evaluation. *Southern Medical Journal* 66: #1, 74–78, January 1973.

Cureton, T. K. *The Physiological Effects of Wheat Germ Oil on Humans in Exercise*. 1972. Springfield, Illinois: Charles C. Thomas.

Currier, W. D. *Dizziness Related to Hypoglycemia: The Role of Adrenal Steroids and Nutrition*. Reprinted from the *Journal of Applied Nutrition* 21: #1 and 2, 1969.

Danowski, T. S. Prevalence of Diabetes. *Medical World News* 8: #22, 17, 2 June 1967.

Diabetes, The Journal of the American Diabetes Association 22: #10, 776–784, October 1973.

Editorial. Diphenylhydantoin and Insulin-Secreting Tumors. *Journal of the American Medical Association* 223: #5, 553–554, 29 January 1973.

Freinkel, N., and Metzger, B. E. Oral Glucose Tolerance Curve and Hypoglycemias in the Fed State. *New England Journal of Medicine* 280: #15, 820–828, 10 April 1969.

Gorman, C. K. Hypoglycemia: A Brief Review. *Medical Clinics of North America* 49: #4, 947–959, July 1965.

Hawkins, D., and Pauling, L. *Orthomolecular Psychiatry, Treatment of Schizophrenia*. 1973. San Francisco: W. H. Freeman and Company.

Mason, C. F. *Hypoglycemia and the Methyl Approach*. Mato Laboratory, P.O. Box 7006, Riverside, California 92503.

Medical News. Coffee's Effect on Diabetes Tested. *Journal of the American Medical Association* 209: #3, 350, 21 July 1969.

National Dairy Council. Lactose Intolerance. *Dairy Council Digest* 42: #6, November–December 1971.

Pfeiffer, E. F., and Ziegler, R. The Prediabetic State. *Triangle* [The Sandoz Journal of Medical Science] 8: #2, 8–16, February 1965.

Prevention Staff. Poor Countries Won't Thank Us for Milk. *Prevention* 23: #8, 133–137, August 1971.

Roberts, S. E. *Exhaustion: Causes and Treatment.* 1967. Emmaus, Pennsylvania: Rodale Books, Inc.

Rodale, J. I. *Natural Health, Sugar and the Criminal Mind.* 1968. Elmhurst, New York: Pyramid Books.

Rorty, J., and Norman, N. *Bio-Organics: Your Food and Your Health.* 1956. Old Greenwich, Connecticut: Devin-Adair Company.

Rosenfeld, C. Nutritional Guidance Can Forestall Broken Marriages. *New Medical Materia*, 51–52, August 1962.

Salzer, H. M. Relative Hypoglycemia as a Cause of Neuropsychiatric Illness. *Journal of the National Medical Association* 58: #1, 12–17, January 1966.

Seltzer, H. S. Drug-Induced Hypoglycemia, a Review of 473 Cases. *Diabetes* 21: #9, 955–966, September 1972.

The Great Medical Debate Over Low Blood Sugar. *Science News* 103: 17, March 1973.

Trace Metals: Medicine's Newest Alchemy: III. A Chromium Key to Glucose Tolerance? *Medical World News* 13: #20, 46–47, 19 May 1972.

The Upjohn Company. *These 52 Factors Can Affect Blood Glucose Levels.* Kalamazoo, Michigan 49001.

You Need Manganese for Good Health. *Better Nutrition*, January 1974.

Yudkin, J. *Sweet and Dangerous.* 1972. New York: Peter H. Wyden, Inc.

CHAPTER SEVEN

Brill, A. A. *Basic Principles of Psychoanalysis.* 1960. New York: Washington Square Press.

Cheraskin, E., and Ringsdorf, W. M., Jr. Daily Tryptophane Consumption and Psychologic State. *Nutrition Reports International* 3: #2, 135–141, February 1971.

Cheraskin, E., Ringsdorf, W. M., Jr., Michael, D. W., and Hicks, B. S. The Relationship of Changes in Daily Tryptophane Consumption to Changes in Psychologic State. *Orthomolecular Psychiatry* 1: #2 & 3, 113–116, Second & Third Quarters, 1972.

Cheraskin, E., Ringsdorf, W. M., Jr., Setyaadmadja, A. T. S. H., and Barrett, R. A. Protein-Nicotinic Acid Consumption and Early

Psychologic Change. *Mental Hygiene* 52: #4, 624–626, October 1968.

Cheraskin, E., Ringsdorf, W. M., Jr., Setyaadmadja, A. T. S. H., and Barrett, R. A. Psychologic Testing [Controlled Association Test] and Protein-Nicotinic Acid Consumption. *Psychiatric Quarterly* 42: #2, 313–320, April 1968.

English, O. S., and Pearson, G. H. J. *Emotional Problems of Living.* 1955. New York: W. W. Norton and Company.

Goldberg, D. P. *The Detection of Psychiatric Illness by Questionnaire.* 1972. London: Oxford University Press.

Green, R. G. Subclinical Pellagra. In Hawkins, D., and Pauling, L. *Orthomolecular Psychiatry; Treatment of Schizophrenia.* 1973. San Francisco: W. H. Freeman and Company.

Hall, R. C. W., and Joffe, J. R. Hypomagnesia: Physical and Psychiatric Symptoms. *J. A. M. A.* 224: #13, 1749–1751, 25 June 1973.

Hawkins, D., and Pauling, L. *Orthomolecular Psychiatry: Treatment of Schizophrenia.* 1973. San Francisco: W. H. Freeman and Company.

Holmes, D. J. *Psychotherapy.* 1972. Boston: Little, Brown and Company.

Pitts, F. N., Jr. The Biochemistry of Anxiety. *Scientific American* 220: #2, 69–75, February 1968.

Rodale, J. I. *Magnesium, the Nutrient That Could Change Your Life.* 1968. Elmhurst, New York: Pyramid Books.

Sharpe, L. *Some Comparisons of American, British and Canadian Psychiatrists in Their Diagnostic Concepts.* Biometrics Research, 722 West 168th Street, New York, New York 10032.

Therapists Warned to Watch for Organic Source of Illness: APA. *Psychiatric News*, 19 September 1973.

Watson, G. *Nutrition and Your Mind.* 1972. New York: Harper and Row.

CHAPTER EIGHT

Adams, P. W., Wynn, V., Rose, D. P., Seed, M., Folkard, J., and Strong, R. Effect of Pyridoxine Hydrochloride [Vitamin B$_6$] Upon Depression Associated with Oral Contraception. *Lancet* 1: #7809, 897–903, 28 April 1973.

Baumblatt, M. J., and Winston, F. Pyridoxine and the Pill. *Lancet* 1: #7651, 832–833, 18 April 1970.

Bennett, A. E., Doll, R., and Howell, R. W. Sugar Consumption and Cigarette Smoking. *Lancet* 1: #7655, 1011–1014, 16 May 1970.

Berman, H. A., and Weinstein, L. Antibiotics and Nutrition. *American Journal of Clinical Nutrition* 24: #2, 260–264, February 1971.

Borquin, A., and Musmanno, E. Preliminary Report on the Effect of Smoking on the Ascorbic Acid Content of Whole Blood. *American Journal of Digestive Diseases* 20: #3, 75–77, March 1953.

Brecher, E. M., and Editors of Consumer Reports. *Licit and Illicit Drugs.* 1972. Mount Vernon, New York: Consumers Union.

Briggs, M., and Briggs, M. Vitamin C Requirements and Oral Contraceptives. *Nature* 238: #5362, 277, 4 August 1972.

Brook, M., and Grimshaw, J. J. Vitamin C Concentration of Plasma and Leukocytes as Relates to Smoking Habit, Age, and Sex of Humans. *American Journal of Clinical Nutrition* 21: #11, 1254–1258, November 1968.

Brown, R. R. Biochemistry and Pathology of Tryptophan, Metabolism and Its Regulation by Amino Acids, Vitamin B₆, and Steroid Hormones. *American Journal of Clinical Nutrition* 24: #2, 243–245, February 1971.

Butterworth, C. E. Correcting Malnutrition: Practical Therapeutic Approaches. *Modern Medicine* 38: #24, 102, 30 November 1970.

Christakis, G., and Miridjanian, A. Diets, Drugs, and Their Interrelationships. *Journal of the American Dietetic Association* 52: #1, 21–24, January 1968.

Editorial. Advice to Women on the Pill: Don't Forget to Take Your Vitamins. *American Druggist Merchandising,* p. 55, 15 January 1973.

Editorial. Drugs to Control Hyperactivity May Slow Children's Growth. *Science News* 103: #15,

Ellis, J. M., and Presley, J. *Vitamin B₆; the Doctor's Report.* 1973. New York: Harper and Row Publishers, Inc.

Food and Drug Administration. *Caffeine.* FDA Fact Sheet #72–3003, July 1971.

Food and Drug Administration. *Tardive Dyskinesia Associated with Antipsychotic Drugs.* FDA Drug Bulletin, May 1973.

Gage, T. W., and Radman, W. P. Drug Interactions: A Professional Responsibility. *Journal of the American Dental Association* 84: #4, 848–853, April 1972.

Guilford, J. S. *Factors Related to Successful Abstinence from Smoking: Final Report.* 1966. Pittsburgh, Pennsylvania.

Goldstein, A., and Kaizer, S. Psychotropic Effects of Caffeine in Man; III. A

Questionnaire Survey of Coffee Drinking and Its Effect in a Group of Housewives. *Clinical Pharmacology and Therapeutics* 10: #4, 477–488, July–August 1969.

Goldstein, A., Kaizer, S., and Whitby, O. Psychotropic Effects of Caffeine in Man. IV. Quantitative and Qualitative Differences Associated with Habituation to Coffee. *Clinical Pharmacology and Therapeutics* 10: #4, 489–497, July–August 1969.

He Treats Addicts by Building Health. *Prevention*   March 1972.

Hoffer, A. *The Drug Addictions, Part One.* The Answer II: 2–5, #4, 1974.

Huff, B. B., and staff. *Physicians' Desk Reference to Pharmaceutical Specialties and Biologicals.* 1973. Oradell, New Jersey: Medical Economics, Inc.

Hussar, D. A. Interactions Involving Drugs Used in Dental Practice. *Journal of the American Dental Association* 87: #2, 349–358, August 1973.

Kane, F. J., Jr., and Lipton, M. Folic Acid and Mental Illness. *Southern Medical Journal* 63: #5, 603–607, May 1970.

Kapp, J. Taking Medicine? You Need B Vitamins. *Prevention* 24: #9, 70–76, September 1972.

Kershbaum, A., Pappajohn, D. J., Bellet, S., Hiraboyashi, M., and Shafiha, H. Effect of Smoking and Nicotine on Adrenocortical Secretion. *Journal of the American Medical Association* 203: #4, 275–278, 22 January 1968.

Mayer, J. Iatrogenic Malnutrition. *Postgraduate Medicine* 49: #3, 247–249, March 1971.

Meyler, L., and Peck, H. M. *Drug Induced Diseases.* Volume 3, 1968. Excerpta Medica Foundation, New York.

Mozdzierz, G. J., Macchitelli, F. J., and Lottman, T. J. Personality Correlates of Coffee Consumption in an Alcoholic Population. *Psychological Reports* 32: #2, 550, April 1973.

Pawlak, V. *Megavitamin Therapy and the Drug Wipeout Syndrome: An Introduction to the Orthomolecular Approach as a Treatment for After-Effects of Drug Use/Abuse.* First Printing, December 1972. Do It Now Foundation, Post Office Box 5115, Phoenix, Arizona 85010.

Pelletier, O. Cigarette Smoking and Vitamin C. *Nutrition Today* 5: #3, 12–15, Autumn 1970.

Reynolds, E. H., Preece, J., and Chanarin, I. Folic Acid and Anticonvulsants. *Lancet* 1: #7609, 1264–1265, 21 June 1969.

Ritchie, J. M., in Goodman, L. S., and Gilman, A. *The Pharmacological Basis of Therapeutics.* Fourth Edition. 1970. p. 359. New York: Macmillan Company.

Rivers, J. M. Plasma Ascorbic Acid Concentrations and Oral Contraceptives. *American Journal of Clinical Nutrition* 25: #7, 684–689, July 1972.

Rodale, R. Large Doses of Aspirin Rob Blood of Vitamin C. *Rodale's Health Bulletin* 9: #12, 1–2, 12 June 1971.

Rodale, R. Oral Contraceptives Implicated in Folic Acid Deficiency. *Rodale's Health Bulletin* 9: #20, 4, 2 October 1971.

Roe, D. A. Nutritional Side Effects of Drugs. *Food and Nutrition News* 45: #1, 1–4, October–November 1973.

Ross, N. M. Avoiding Drug Interactions. *Journal of Oral Medicine* 28: #3, 73–76, July–September 1973.

Russell, M. A. H. Cigarette Smoking: Natural History of a Dependence Disorder. *British Journal of Medical Psychology* 44: Part 1, 1–16, March 1971.

Sahud, M. A., and Cohen, R. J. Effect of Aspirin Ingestion on Ascorbic-Acid Levels in Rheumatoid Arthritis. *Lancet* 1: #7706, 937–938, 8 May 1971.

Samter, M. Drug Antigens and the Diseases Which They Produce. *Transactions and Studies of the College of Physicians of Philadelphia* 33: #3, 171–179, January 1966.

Schwartz, H. A. Doctor: Here Are Tests to Help You Prepare Your Patients for Quitting the Cigarette Habit. *Medical Bulletin on Tobacco* 7: #4, Winter 1969–1970.

Shojania, A. M., Hornady, G., and Barnes, P. H. Oral Contraceptives and Serum-Folate Level. *Lancet* 1: #7656, 1376–1377, 22 June 1968.

Shatz, A., and Shatz, V. One Puff of Death. *Prevention* 23: #11, 168–172, November 1972.

Taub, H. J. Tetracycline Therapy Can Backfire in Elderly by Depleting Vitamin C. *Rodale's Health Bulletin* 10: #6, 1, 18 March 1972.

Wertalik, L. F., Metz, E. N., Lobuglio, A. F., and Balcerzak, S. P. Decreased serum B_{12} Levels Secondary to Oral Contraceptive Agents. *American Journal of Clinical Nutrition* 24: #5, 603, May 1971.

Yaryura-Tobias, J. A. L-Dopa and Mental Illness. *Orthomolecular Psychiatry* 1: #2–3, 133–136, Second and Third Quarter, 1972.

CHAPTER NINE

Altman, H., Mehta, D., Evenson, R. C., and Sletten, I. W. Behavioral Effects of Drug Therapy on Psychogeriatric Inpatients. II. Multivitamin Supplement. *Journal of the American Geriatrics Society* 21: #6, 249–252, June 1973.

Boyle, E., Jr. Reversal of Memory Loss by Hyperbaric Oxygen. In Summit, L., *The Crisis of Health Care for the Aging.* Report of a National Conference by The Huxley Institute for Biosocial Research, New York City. 6 March 1972.

Coca, A. F. *The Pulse Test.* New York: Arco Books, Inc.

Cott, A. Orthomolecular Approach to the Treatment of Learning Disabilities. *Schizophrenia* 3: #2, 95–105, Second Quarter 1971.

Cott, A. Reflections by an Orthomolecular Psychiatrist. *Orthomolecular Psychiatry* 2: #3, 104-105, Third Quarter 1973.

Feingold, B. F. Adverse Reactions to Food Additives. Proceedings, American Medical Association Convention, June 1973.

Feingold, B. F. Food Additives and Child Development. *Hospital Practice* 8: #9, 11–12, 17–18, 21, October 1973.

Fredericks, C. *Eating Right for You.* 1972. New York: Grosset and Dunlap.

Hoffer, A. Senility Is a Form of Chronic Malnutrition. In Summit, L., *The Crisis of Health Care for the Aging.* Report of a National Conference by The Huxley Institute for Biosocial Research, New York City. 6 March 1972.

Levitt, E. E. The Results of Psychotherapy with Children: An Evaluation. *Journal of Consulting Psychology* 21: #3, 189–196, 1957.

Loeb, M. B., and Howell, S. C. Nutrition and Aging: A Monograph for Practitioners. *The Gerontologist* 9: #3, Part II, Autumn 1969.

Mandell, M. Cerebral Reactions in Allergic Patients. Second International Congress of Social Psychiatry, Section on Ecological Mental Illness, London, England. 8 August 1969.

Mandell, M. An Introduction to Ecological Mental Illness: Demonstrable Cerebral Reactions from Foods and Chemical Exposures: A Motion Picture Documentation. *Review of Allergy* 23 #11, November 1969.

Mitra, M. L. Confusional States in Relation to Vitamin Deficiencies in the Elderly. *Journal of the American Geriatrics Society* 19: #6, 536–545, June 1971.

Newbold, H. L., Philpott, W. H., and Mandell M. Psychiatric Syndromes Produced by Allergies: Ecological Mental Illness. *Orthomolecular Psychiatry* 2: #3, 84–92, Third Quater 1973.

Rees, E. L. Clinical Observations on the Treatment of Schizophrenic and Hyperactive Children with Megavitamins. *Orthomolecular Psychiatry* 2: #3, 92–103, Third Quater 1973.

Rimland, B. *Freud Is Dead: New Directions in the Treatment of Mentally Ill Children.* University of Southern California, Distinguished Lecture Series in Special Education, June 1970.

Rimland, B. Psychogenesis versus Biogenesis: The Issues and the Evidence. In Plog, S. C., and Edgerton, R. B. *Changing Perspectives in Mental Illness.* 1969. New York: Holt, Rinehart and Winston.

Smith, C. J. Non-hormonal Control of Vaso-motor Flushing in Menopausal Patients. *Chicago Medicine* 67: #5, 193–195, 7 March 1964.

Vitamins for Your Child's Intelligence. *Prevention* magazine, August 1968.

Whanger, A. D. Vitamins and Vigor at 65 Plus. *Postgraduate Medicine* 53: #2, 167–172, February 1973.

CHAPTER TEN

AMA Committee on Exercise and Physical Fitness. Is Your Patient Fit? *The Journal of the American Medical Association* 201: #2, 117–118, 10 July 1967.

Arvidsson, O., Johannsson, C. R., Olsson, K., and Wigeman, H. Community Noise: A Sociological-Psychological Study. *Nordisk Hygienisk Tidskrift* 46: #4, 153–188, 1965.

Anti-Crowd Weapon Works by Causing Fits. *New Scientist.* p. 726. 29 March 1973.

Benning, D. Outbreak of Mercury Poisoning in Ohio. *Industrial Medicine and Surgery* 27: #7, 354–363, 1958.

Brown, R. New Worries About Unheard Sound. *New Scientist.* pp. 414–415. 8 November 1973.

Cheraskin, E., and Ringsdorf, W. M., Jr. *Predictive Medicine; A Study in Strategy.* 1973. Mountain View, California: Pacific Press Publishing Association.

Cheraskin, E., Ringsdorf, W. M., Jr., Michael, D. W., and Hicks, B. S. The Exercise Profile. *Journal of the American Geriatrics Society* 21: #5, 208–215, May 1973.

Chowns, R. H. Mental-Hospital Admissions and Aircraft Noise. *Lancet* 1: #7644, 467, 1970.

Cook, R. K. Strange Sounds in the Atmosphere. *Sound* 1: #2, 12–16, March–April 1962.

Cooper, K. H., Gey, G. O., and Bottenberg, R. A. Effects of Cigarette Smoking on Endurance Performance. *The Journal of the American Medical Association* 203: #3, 189–192, 15 January 1968.

Cureton, T. K. *The Physiological Effects of Wheat Germ Oil on Humans in Exercise.* 1972. Springfield, Illinois: Charles C. Thomas.

Gallager, J. R. *Medical Care of the Adolescent.* Second edition. 1966. New York: Appleton-Century-Crofts, Inc.

Geller, I. Ethanol Preference in the Rat as a Function of Photoperiod. *Science* 173: #3995, 456–459, 30 July 1973.

Goerke, V. H. Private communication.

Green, J., Bell Telephone Laboratories, Napier, Illinois. Private communication.

Green, J. E., and Dunn F. Correlation of Naturally Occurring Infrasonics and Selected Human Behavior. *The Journal of the Acoustical Society of America* 44: #5, 1456–1457, November 1968.

Hammond, E. C. Some Preliminary Findings on Physical Complaints from a Prospective Study of 1,064,004 Men and Women. *American Journal of Public Health* 54: #1, 11–23, January 1964.

Incinerator Still Belching Mercury into D.C. Skies. *Washington Star-News*, 13 March 1974.

Jogging for Juicers. *Human Behavior.* December 1973.

Kraus, H. Evaluation of Muscular and Cardiovascular Fitness. *Preventive Medicine* 1: #1–2, 178–184, March 1972.

Laverne, A. Nonspecific Air-Pollution Syndrome [NAPS]. *Behavioral Neuropsychiatry* 2: #7, 19–21, 1970.

Mandell, M. *Ecologic, Allergic and Metabolic Factors in the Etiology of Physical and Mental Disorders. New Dynamics of Preventive Medicine.* 1974. New York: Intercontinental Medical Book Corporation.

National Dairy Council. Nutrition and Physical Fitness. *Dairy Council Digest* 36: #5, September–October 1965.

Ott, J. N. *Health and Light; The Effects of Natural and Artificial Light on Man and Other Living Things.* 1973. Old Greenwich, Connecticut: The Devin-Adair Company.

Pollution: Its Impact on Mental Health. National Institute of Mental Health. DHEW Publication No. [HSM] 72-9135.

Sharon, I. M., Feller, R. P., and Burney, S. W. The Effects of Lights of Different Spectra on Caries Incidence in the Golden Hamster. *Archives of Oral Biology* 16: #12, 1427–1432, December 1971.

Temple, J. Strange Sounds in the Atmosphere. *ESSA World,* U.S. Department of Commerce Environmental Science Services Administration, January 1969. pp. 24–26.

Wurtman, R. J., and Neer, R. M. Good Light and Bad. *The New England Journal of Medicine* 282: #7, 394–395, 12 February 1970.

CHAPTER ELEVEN

Cheraskin, E., and Ringsdorf, W. M., Jr. Daily Phenylalanine Consumption and Psychologic State. *Nutrition Reports International* 3: #6, 377–382, June 1971.

Cheraskin, E., and Ringsdorf, W. M., Jr. Daily Tryptophane Consumption and Psychologic State. *Nutrition Reports International* 3: #2, 135–141, February 1971.

Cheraskin, E., and Ringsdorf, W. M., Jr. Familial Factors in Psychic Adjustment. *Journal of the American Geriatric Society* 17: #6, 609–611, June 1969.

Cheraskin, E., and Ringsdorf, W. M., Jr. Mental Illness Proneness Profile. *Alabama Journal of Medical Sciences* 10: #1, 32–45, January 1973.

Cheraskin, E., Ringsdorf, W. M., Jr., Michael, D. W., and Hicks, B. S. The Relationship of Changes in Daily Tryptophane Consumption to Changes in Psychologic State. *Orthomolecular Psychiatry* 1: #2–3, 113–116, Second and Third Quarters, 1972.

Cheraskin, E., Ringsdorf, W. M., Jr., Setyaadmadja, A. T. S. H., and Barrett, R. A. Protein-Nicotinic Acid Consumption and Early Psychologic Change. *Mental Hygiene* 52: #4, 624–626, October 1968.

Cheraskin, E., Ringsdorf, W. M., Jr., Setyaadmadja, A. T. S. H., and Barrett, R. A. Psychologic Testing [Controlled Association Test] and Protein-Nicotinic Acid Consumption. *Psychiatric Quarterly* 42: #2, 313–320, April 1968.

Zung, W. W. K. A Rating Instrument for Anxiety Disorders. *Psychosomatics* 12: #6, 371–379, November–December 1971.

CHAPTER TWELVE

Alvarez, W. C. Are Americans Pill Takers? *The Birmingham News.* Tuesday, 3 October 1972.

Bieler, H. G. *Food Is Your Best Medicine.* 1966. New York: Random House, Inc.

Briggs, G. M. Cited by Fordham, K. C., and Condos, R. C., in *Prevention of Disease Through Proper Nutrition.* 1972. Anro, Inc., Box M., Devon, Pennsylvania 19333.

Brodman, K., Erdmann, A. J., Jr., and Wolff, H. G. *Cornell Medical Index Health Questionnaire Manual.* 1949. Cornell University Medical College, 1300 York Avenue, New York, New York.

Cheraskin, E., and Ringsdorf, W. M., Jr. *New Hope for Incurable Diseases.* 1971. Jericho, New York: Exposition Press.

Cheraskin, E., Ringsdorf, W. M., Jr., and Clark, J. W. *Diet and Disease.* 1968. Emmaus, Pennsylvania: Rodale Books.

Clark, J. W., Cheraskin, E., and Ringsdorf, W. M., Jr. *Diet and the Periodontal Patient.* 1970. Springfield, Illinois: Charles C. Thomas.

Dietronics, Division of Hanson Research Corporation, Post Office Box 35, 19727 Bahama Street, Northridge, California 91324.

Editorial. Nutrition Pot-Pourri; Heating Causes Nutrient Losses. *Food and Nutrition News* 41: #7, 2, April 1970.

Frank E. Greene and Son, Inc. *Fortified Sugars.* 3537 West Pershing Road, Chicago, Illinois 60632.

Harris, R. S., and Loesecke, H. V. *Nutritional Evaluation of Food Processing.* 1960. New York: John Wiley and Sons.

Hearings before the Committee on Interstate and Foreign Commerce of the United States House of Representatives and its Subcommittee on Public Health and Environment, Washington, D.C., October 1973.

Highlights from the Ten-State Nutrition Survey. *Nutrition Today* 7: #4, 4–11, July–August 1972.

Marks, J. *The Vitamins in Health and Disease: A Modern Reappraisal.* 1968. London: J. and A. Churchill, Ltd.

CHAPTER THIRTEEN

American Dental Association. *Diet and Dental Health.* 211 East Chicago Avenue, Chicago, Illinois 60611.

Cheraskin, E., Ringsdorf, W. M., Jr., and Clark, J. W. *Diet and Disease.* 1968. Emmaus, Pennsylvania: Rodale Press.

Clark, J. W., Cheraskin, E., and Ringsdorf, W. M., Jr. *Diet and the Periodontal Patient.* 1970. Springfield, Illinois: Charles C. Thomas.

Feingold, B. F. Food Additives and Child Development. *Hospital Practice* 8: #9, 11–12, 17–18, 21, October 1973.

Hall, R. L. Food Additives. *Nutrition Today* 8: #4, 20–28, July–August 1973.

Jacobson, M. *Nutrition Scoreboard; Your Guide to Better Eating.* 1973. Center for Science in the Public Interest, 1779 Church Street N.W., Washington, D.C. 20036.

National Dairy Council. *A Guide to Good Eating.* 111 North Canal Street, Chicago, Illinois 60606.

Pauling, L. *Vitamin C and the Common Cold.* 1970. San Francisco: W. H. Freeman and Company.

Raiford, M. Panel Discussion, International Academy of Preventive Medicine Convention, October 1973.

Sharp, G. S., and Fister, H. W. The Diagnosis and Treatment of Achlorhydria: A Ten Year Study. *Journal of the American Geriatrics Society* 15: #8, 786–791, August 1967.

Sheraton, M. Junk Food. *Diversion* 2: #1, 37–64, February 1974.

United States Department of Agriculture. *Food for Fitness: A Daily Food Guide.* Leaflet #424.

Wilson, C. Vitamin C and the Common Cold. *Saturday Evening Post* 246: #3, 34–35, April 1974.

Index